Costa Rica Travel Guide 2024

Step-by-Step Itineraries, Local Secrets, and Eco-Friendly Explorations for a Transformative Costa Rican Experience

SARA PALMA

DEDICATION

To my family, whose love and support make every trip possible. To my friends, who share travel memories and stories with me. To the people of Costa Rica, who are so warm and welcoming. To all travelers, I hope this guide helps you explore and enjoy the beauty of the world. And to you, the reader, thank you for reading my book and seeing Costa Rica through my eyes. Pura Vida!

Copyright and Disclaimer

Legal Notice

Disclaimer Notice

CONTENTS

INTRODUCTION

Costa Rica, a small but amazing country in Central America with lush rainforests, beautiful beaches, and incredible wildlife. You can hear waves crashing and birds singing. This place is a natural paradise for sure.

Costa Rica has no army. It decided to focus on peace, education, and protecting nature. Even though it is small, it has more than 5% of the world's plants and animals. Everywhere you look, you will see unique plants and animals.

People visit for many reasons. If you like adventure, you can zip-line through the forest, raft on wild rivers, or surf big waves at the beach. You will enjoy the national parks with sloths, toucans, and maybe even jaguars. If you want to relax, there are beautiful beaches and hot springs.

To really enjoy your trip, stay for about 10 to 14 days. Start in San José, the capital. Visit museums and lively markets. Then go to the Pacific coast for sun and surf. Explore the Central Valley with its coffee farms and volcanoes. Then, visit the Caribbean coast for a different culture and relaxed vibe.

Spanish is the main language as you may know already, but many people speak English, especially in tourist areas. The locals, called Ticos, are friendly and welcoming.

Costa Rica is small, about the size of West Virginia in the United States. It has many different landscapes and climates. It is special because it protects its environment. The government and people work hard to keep nature pristine.

This Country became independent from Spain in 1821. It is one of the most stable and prosperous countries in Latin America. It focuses on education and healthcare, making people happy and healthy.

Costa Rica became popular from travel shows and documentaries. What you see on TV—the beautiful landscapes, wildlife, and adventures—is what you get when you visit. The reality is even better.

After visiting, many travelers go to nearby countries like Nicaragua or Panama. But, also Belize has more to offer. These places are also beautiful, but Costa Rica is unique with its mix of adventure, nature, and friendly people.

1. Land of Pura Vida

Costa Rica

This country is a small, beautiful place in Central America, right between Nicaragua and Panama. To the east, it has the Caribbean Sea, and to the west, it has the Pacific Ocean. The land here is full of different kinds of nature, from sunny beaches to green rainforests.

There are seven main areas, called provinces: San José, Alajuela, Cartago, Heredia, Guanacaste, Puntarenas, and Limón. Each one is special in its own way. In the middle of the country, you will find the capital city, San José. This city is in a valley, surrounded by tall mountains like the Central Cordillera and the Talamanca Mountains. You can see big volcanoes here, like Poás, Irazú, and Arenal.

If you go west, you will reach the Pacific coast. This side of the country is sunny and dry, especially in Guanacaste. People call this area the "Gold Coast" because of its golden beaches and fun places to stay. You can surf, swim, or just relax and watch the beautiful sunset over the ocean.

On the other side, to the east, is the Caribbean coast. This area is more humid and full of green plants. Limón is the main province here. The culture is rich with Afro-Caribbean music, festivals, and delicious food. The rainforests are home to many animals, like howler monkeys, sloths, colorful birds, and butterflies.

This country is famous for its amazing wildlife. Even though it is small, as i told you before it has about 5% of all the species in the world. You can see different kinds of forests, like rainforests, dry forests, and cloud forests. There are also mangrove swamps and coral reefs. Each type of forest has its own special plants and animals.

The Monteverde Cloud Forest Reserve is a magical place high up in the mountains. It is misty and green, with many types of plants, birds, and animals. Walking through this forest feels like being in a fairy tale, with vines hanging down and birds singing all around.

The Osa Peninsula, in the south, is another amazing place. It has Corcovado National Park, which is one of the most biodiverse spots on the planet. You can hike through thick jungles, see rare animals like jaguars, and enjoy quiet, untouched beaches.

For marine life lovers, Marino Ballena National Park on the Pacific coast is a must-see. It is named for its whale-tail-shaped beach and is known for whale watching. Every year, humpback whales come here to have their babies. On the Caribbean side, Cahuita National Park has beautiful coral reefs where you can snorkel and see colorful fish, sea turtles, and even nurse sharks

Why Costa Rica? Why Not!

There are many reasons to visit this beautiful country. The beaches are amazing, with golden sands and clear blue water. You can surf, swim, or just relax in the sun. The rainforests are full of life. You can see monkeys, sloths, colorful birds, and butterflies. There are many national parks where you can hike and explore. Monteverde Cloud Forest Reserve and Corcovado National

Park are top spots for nature lovers.

Active volcanoes are another big draw. Arenal Volcano is a must-see, with hot springs nearby where you can relax. Poás Volcano has a big, beautiful crater that is easy to reach.

If you like adventures, there are lots of activities. You can zip-line through the forest, go white-water rafting, or scuba dive in the ocean. It's perfect for outdoor fun.

The people here are friendly and welcoming. They have a saying, "Pura Vida," which means "Pure Life." It shows their happy and relaxed way of living.

The food is delicious and fresh. Try "casado," a traditional dish with rice, beans, plantains, salad, and meat. Fresh fruits like pineapples, mangoes, and bananas are everywhere.

The weather is warm all year. There are two main seasons: the dry season from December to April and the rainy season from May to November. Even in the rainy season, it doesn't rain all the time, so you can still enjoy your trip.

History

In 1502, Christopher Columbus arrived on the eastern coast during his fourth voyage to the New World. This marked the beginning of Spanish interest in the area. In 1561, Spanish settlers founded the city of Cartago, which became the first capital. The Spanish ruled for nearly 300 years, influencing the culture and architecture. In 1821, the country gained independence from Spain, along with the rest of Central America. The news of independence reached the country a month later. In 1824, San José became the new capital, replacing Cartago after a brief civil conflict between cities. In 1848, the nation officially became a republic. Juan Mora Fernández was the first head of state, leading the country through early years of independence. In 1856, national hero Juan Santamaría played a key role in the Battle of Rivas, fighting against American filibuster William Walker who tried to conquer Central America. Santamaría's bravery is celebrated every year on April 11th.

In 1948, after a disputed presidential election, a civil war broke out. José Figueres Ferrer led the victorious rebel forces. Following the conflict, he abolished the military and established a new constitution in 1949.

Since then, the country has enjoyed peace and stability, focusing on education, healthcare, and environmental protection, becoming a model for democracy in the region.

Today, it is known for its strong democracy, lack of military, and commitment to conservation. The country continues to thrive, welcoming visitors from all over the world.

What You Need to Know

Almost everybody can visit for up to 90 days without needing a visa. Check with your local embassy to confirm this and ensure your passport is valid for at least six months from your entry date.

The local currency is the colón. You can exchange money at banks, hotels, and airports, but local banks offer the best rates. ATMs are widely available and accept major credit cards like Visa and MasterCard. Keep some local currency on hand for small purchases, though credit cards are accepted in most places.

Spanish is the official language, so knowing basic phrases like "Hola" (Hello), "Gracias" (Thank you), and "Por favor" (Please) is helpful. Many people in tourist areas speak some English, but making an effort with Spanish will enhance your experience.

For emergencies, dial 911 for police, medical help, and the fire department. The Tourist Police, who are very helpful, can be reached at 800-887-4766. Save these numbers on your phone.

Healthcare is excellent, with both public and private hospitals, especially in San José. Travel insurance that covers medical expenses is highly recommended to avoid any costly surprises if you need medical treatment.

Electricity is 110 volts, like in the U.S., so you won't need a voltage converter if you're coming from there. Bring a plug adapter if your devices use different plugs to ensure you can charge everything.

Tap water is generally safe to drink, but it's wise to ask locals if you're unsure. Bottled water is cheap and widely available, so staying hydrated is easy.

Public buses are the cheapest way to get around and cover most destinations. Taxis are common; ensure the driver uses the meter or agree on a fare before starting your trip. If you prefer driving, renting a car is a good option. Just be prepared for narrow roads and occasional wildlife.

Always carry a copy of your passport and keep the original in your hotel's safe to prevent any issues if your documents get lost or stolen.

Vaccinations are not required, but it's smart to check with your doctor before traveling. Vaccines for hepatitis A, typhoid, and sometimes malaria are recommended, especially if you're visiting rural areas.

For packing, bring light, breathable clothing for the warm weather and rain gear if you're traveling during the rainy season from May to November. Sun protection is crucial, so pack sunscreen, a hat, and sunglasses.

Most hotels and cafes offer free Wi-Fi. If you need internet on the go, buying a local SIM card is easy. Head to a store like Kolbi, Movistar, or Claro. Bring your passport, as you'll need it to register the SIM. The process is quick, and the staff usually speak some English. SIM cards are inexpensive, and you can top them up with prepaid credit at most convenience stores or kiosks.

The time zone is Central Standard Time, with no daylight saving time, so it's the same as Chicago year-round, making it simple to adjust your schedule.

Cultural Insights: The Heart of Costa Rica

"Pura Vida" is a phrase you'll hear everywhere. It means "Pure Life" and people use it to say hello, goodbye, and to show they are happy. It reflects the relaxed and positive way of life here.

Family is very important. On weekends, families gather for big meals with lots of talking and laughing. If you get invited, it's a special experience.

Christmas is a big celebration with lights, nativity scenes, and fireworks at midnight on Christmas Eve. During Holy Week, or Semana Santa, there are many religious parades and ceremonies, and people spend time with family. Independence Day on September 15th is celebrated with parades, music, and dances. Everyone wears the national colors—red, white, and blue—and waves the flag proudly. Politeness is key. Always say "Buenos días" for good morning, "Buenas tardes" for good afternoon, or "Buenas noches" for good night when you meet someone. Use "Señor" for Mr. and "Señora" for Mrs. to show respect. Friends and family greet each other with a light kiss on the cheek.

When you visit someone's home, bring a small gift like flowers or dessert to show your thanks. In restaurants, a 10% tip is standard and often included in the bill, but it's good to check. People are relaxed about time. If things start a bit late, it's normal. This easy-going attitude helps create a stress-free environment.

2. San José

How to Get There Without Losing Your Mind

To get to San José, fly into Juan Santamaría International Airport, which is about 20 kilometers from downtown. Most international flights land here. After you land, you have several ways to get to your hotel or wherever you're staying. Taxis are right outside the terminal. Look for the official red ones with a yellow triangle. Make sure the driver uses the meter, which locals call the "María." If you want to save money, take the bus. The bus stop is just outside the airport on the main road. Buses run frequently and are cheap.

Once you're in the city, getting around is easy. Public buses are everywhere and cost very little. They can get crowded, especially during rush hour, but they run from early morning until late at night. Taxis are another good option. Always check that the driver uses the meter. You can also use ridesharing apps like Uber, which are popular and often more comfortable.

If you like driving, you can rent a car. There are many car rental agencies at the airport and in the city. Driving here can be tricky because of the traffic and narrow streets. Using a GPS or a reliable map app will help a lot.

In downtown San José, many attractions, restaurants, and shops are close together, so walking is a good way to get around. The streets are busy, so be careful when crossing.

Top Attractions

The Grand National Theatre

The Grand National Theatre, known as Teatro Nacional, opened in 1897. It was built during the coffee boom when wealthy coffee barons wanted a grand place for the arts. This theatre was financed by the government and private citizens who wanted a cultural landmark.

The architecture is a mix of neoclassical and baroque styles. Outside, you'll see statues of Beethoven and Calderón de la Barca. The building itself is elegant with intricate details. Inside, the theatre is even more stunning. Italian marble floors, gold leaf decorations, and rich artwork adorn the space. The ceiling mural, "Allegory of Coffee and Bananas," by Aleardo Villa, celebrates the importance of coffee and bananas to the economy. The colors and imagery are vibrant and symbolic.

Over the years, the theater has hosted many famous performers. Enrico Caruso, the Italian tenor, and Anna Pavlova, the Russian ballerina, are among the legends who have performed here. The acoustics are exceptional, making every performance memorable. The theatre remains a premier cultural venue, offering a variety of shows including classical concerts, opera, and local theatre.

Guided tours are available for those interested in the history and architecture. These tours offer an in-depth look at the theatre's construction, artwork, and the stories behind them. Walking through the grand halls and sitting in the auditorium, you can sense the vibrant cultural life that has thrived here for over a century.

The Shiny Pre-Columbian Gold Museum

The Pre-Columbian Gold Museum, hidden beneath the lively Plaza de la Cultura, is a must-visit. It houses over 1,600 gold artifacts from 500 AD to 1500 AD, offering a fascinating glimpse into ancient indigenous life and craftsmanship. The intricate gold jewelry is stunning. You'll see earrings, necklaces, and bracelets, all finely crafted with detailed designs that show incredible skill. These pieces are not just beautiful; they tell stories of their wearers and the ceremonies they were part of.

Animal figurines made entirely of gold are another highlight. These small sculptures depict frogs, eagles, and jaguars, each significant in indigenous mythology and daily life. The detail is amazing, bringing these ancient beliefs to life.

Ceremonial items, including gold masks and breastplates worn by chiefs and warriors, showcase their spiritual significance and power. The masks have intricate patterns and designs, reflecting the ceremonial importance and artistry involved.

Tools and ornaments highlight advanced goldsmithing techniques. You can see how the indigenous peoples shaped gold into complex forms, using sophisticated methods for their time.

The museum is open daily from 9:15 AM to 5:00 PM. Admission is affordable, with discounts for students, children, and seniors. Guided tours provide deeper insights into the exhibits, explaining the cultural and historical context behind the artifacts.

The Mysterious Jade Museum

The Jade Museum, right in the heart of downtown San José, is an absolute must-see for anyone keen on delving into the rich and fascinating history of ancient civilizations. This museum boasts the world's largest collection of pre-Columbian jade artifacts, with pieces dating from 500 BC to 800 AD, offering a stunning display of the exceptional craftsmanship of the indigenous peoples who once inhabited this region.

Getting to the Jade Museum is quite straightforward. If you're staying in the city center, you can easily walk there, as it's located at the Plaza de la Democracia, a notable landmark in San José. For those staying a bit farther out, taxis and rideshare services like Uber are reliable and convenient options to reach the museum. Simply tell the driver "Museo del Jade," and they will know exactly where to take you. If you prefer using public transportation, many bus routes pass through downtown San José, and you can ask the driver to drop you off near the museum.

Once you step inside, you will be captivated by the extensive array of jade artifacts that tell the story of ancient times. The collection includes an impressive selection of jade jewelry, such as necklaces, earrings, and pendants, each intricately designed with detailed patterns that highlight the incredible skill of the ancient artisans. These pieces are not just decorative; they represent the deep cultural significance and the high status of jade in ancient society.

The museum also features a variety of tools and weapons made from jade, underscoring its importance not just as ornamental but also as a functional material in daily life and ceremonial practices. These artifacts provide a window into the everyday activities and the ceremonial rituals of the people who crafted and used them.

One of the most fascinating aspects of the museum is its collection of jade animal figurines. These small sculptures depict various creatures, such as frogs, birds, and jaguars, each with symbolic meanings tied to the mythology and beliefs of the ancient cultures. The detail in these figurines is astounding, offering a vivid glimpse into the symbolic world of these ancient civilizations.

The jade masks are another highlight of the museum. These masks, used in a range of rituals and ceremonies, are masterpieces of ancient art and craftsmanship. Each mask is adorned with intricate patterns and designs that reflect the spiritual and ceremonial life of the people who made and used them. These masks provide deep insight into the religious and cultural practices of the time.

The museum itself is housed in a modern, well-designed building with spacious galleries that allow you to appreciate the artifacts up close. Each exhibit is thoughtfully arranged to tell a story, guiding you through the history and significance of jade in a way that is both informative and engaging.

The Jade Museum is open daily from 8:00 AM to 5:00 PM, making it easy to fit a visit into your schedule. The admission fees are quite reasonable, with discounts available for students, children, and seniors, ensuring that the museum is accessible to all.

The Colorful Central Market

The Central Market, or Mercado Central, sits on Avenida Central between Calles 6 and 8, right in the heart of San José. If you're staying downtown, it's an easy walk. For those farther out, taking a taxi or a bus to Avenida Central will get you there quickly.

As soon as you enter, you're greeted by a maze of narrow aisles filled with vibrant stalls. Start at the fruit stands, where you'll find a variety of exotic fruits like mangos, papayas, and guavas. Be sure to try "mango verde con sal y limón," a local favorite of green mango with salt and lime. The taste is refreshing and tangy, perfect for a quick snack.

Moving deeper into the market, you'll discover small food stalls serving traditional dishes. "Casado," which includes rice, beans, plantains, salad, and a choice of meat, is a must-try. These meals are delicious and affordable, giving you a real taste of local cuisine. Don't miss the ceviche, a marinated seafood dish that's fresh and bursting with flavor.

Shopping in the market is a unique experience. Look for the artisan stalls selling handmade goods. You'll find woven bags, colorful hammocks, and traditional pottery. These items make perfect souvenirs and reflect the rich cultural heritage. Leather goods are another highlight, with vendors offering high-quality wallets, belts, and bags.

Herbs and spices are abundant in the market. The aromas of fresh herbs and spices fill the air, and you can buy everything you need to recreate local dishes at home. Coffee, one of the country's most famous exports, is available in many forms, from whole beans to ground coffee. It's a great idea to buy some to take home.

The Central Market has been a bustling part of the city since 1880, making it a place of cultural significance. It's more than just a shopping destination; it's a window into daily life. Walking through the market, you can interact with locals, see their everyday activities, and understand more about their way of life. It's a place where the vibrant culture comes alive, offering a deeper connection to the traditions and customs of the people.

Best Accommodations

If you're looking for luxury, the Gran Hotel Costa Rica, located on Avenida Central and Calle 2, is a fantastic choice. This historic hotel offers elegant rooms with all the modern amenities you'd expect from a top-tier establishment. Its prime location right in the heart of the city makes it an ideal base for exploring San José. You can easily reach the hotel by taxi from the airport or any part of the city. The hotel itself is steeped in history and charm, with beautiful architecture and a rooftop terrace that offers stunning views of the cityscape.

Another luxurious option is Hotel Grano de Oro, situated on Calle 30, between Avenidas 2 and 4. This boutique hotel features beautifully decorated rooms, each with unique character and style. The on-site restaurant is renowned for its gourmet cuisine, making it a perfect place to enjoy a special meal. The hotel is within walking distance of many attractions, and taxis from the airport or other parts of the city will get you there without any hassle.

For those who want a more contemporary luxury experience, consider the InterContinental Costa Rica at Multiplaza Mall. Located in the upscale neighborhood of Escazú, this hotel offers luxurious rooms, multiple dining options, and a large pool area. It's just a short drive from downtown San José and easily accessible by taxi or rideshare services.

For a comfortable mid-range stay, consider the Park Inn by Radisson, located at Avenida 6, Calle 28. This hotel offers modern rooms, a lovely pool, and a fitness center. Its location is convenient for both business and leisure travelers, being a short taxi ride from both the airport and downtown. The neighborhood is safe and has several dining options nearby, making it a practical choice for visitors.

Hotel Presidente, on Avenida Central, Calle 7, is another great mid-range option. This hotel provides stylish, modern rooms and a rooftop bar with panoramic views of the city. Its central location means you can easily explore many of San José's attractions on foot, and taxis are readily available for longer trips. The hotel's blend of comfort and convenience makes it a favorite among travelers.

If you're looking for a mid-range hotel with a bit more local charm, try the Fleur de Lys Hotel on Calle 13, between Avenidas 2 and 6. This charming hotel is set in a converted Victorian mansion and offers a unique, cozy atmosphere with beautifully decorated rooms and a quaint garden area.

For budget accommodations, Selina San José, located on Avenida 9, Calle 13, is a popular choice. This vibrant hostel offers a range of options from dormitory beds to private rooms, catering to different budget levels. The atmosphere is lively, with frequent events and a social vibe that's perfect for meeting other travelers. It's within walking distance of many downtown attractions, and taxis or buses can get you there quickly if you're coming from the airport.

Another budget-friendly option is Casa 69, located on Calle 25 bis, between Avenidas 6 and 8. This cozy bed and breakfast offers comfortable rooms with a homely feel. The owners are very welcoming and provide personal attention to guests, making it a lovely place to stay. It's a short taxi ride from the city center, and the surrounding area is peaceful, providing a relaxing retreat after a day of exploring.

If you're traveling on a tight budget but still want a central location, Hostel Pangea on Calle 7, between Avenidas 9 and 11, is a great option. It offers dormitory and private rooms, a rooftop bar, and a pool. It's close to many attractions and easily reachable by taxi or bus.

When it comes to choosing a neighborhood, Barrio Amón is a top recommendation for its historical charm and proximity to museums, art galleries, and a variety of restaurants. The area is perfect for walking and soaking up the local culture, with its beautifully preserved colonial buildings and leafy streets.

Escalante is another excellent neighborhood, especially for food lovers and nightlife enthusiasts. This area is known for its trendy cafes, gourmet restaurants, and vibrant bar scene. It's also very walkable, with plenty of options to explore on foot, and taxis are readily available for getting around.

Sabana Norte is also worth considering. It's a bit quieter and more residential, but it's close to La Sabana Metropolitan Park, the largest urban park in San José. Here, you'll find several mid-range and budget hotels, and it's a great area for those who enjoy green spaces and a more relaxed atmosphere.

Dining and Nightlife: Feast and Frolic

For an unforgettable fine dining experience, you must visit Restaurante Grano de Oro, located on Calle 30. This exquisite restaurant, part of the charming Hotel Grano de Oro, is renowned for its French and tropical fusion cuisine. The atmosphere is elegant and intimate, making it perfect for a special evening out. The menu features delicacies like duck confit, seared tuna, and their famous tres leches dessert, all presented with impeccable attention to detail. You can easily reach this gem by taxi from any part of the city, and it's well worth the journey.

Another top culinary destination is Park Cafe on Avenida de Las Americas. This restaurant, set within a beautiful antique gallery, offers a unique dining experience with a blend of European and local dishes. The focus here is on high-quality, fresh ingredients, and the chef's tasting menu is a highlight. Each dish is a work of art, from the delicate seafood platters to the rich, flavorful meats. The intimate setting and superb service make it a memorable spot for dinner.

For a taste of authentic local cuisine, head to Soda Tapia, conveniently located next to La Sabana Metropolitan Park on Avenida Central. This casual eatery has been a favorite among locals for decades, serving up hearty traditional dishes. Try the gallo pinto for breakfast, a satisfying mix of rice and beans often served with eggs and sour cream. For lunch or dinner, the casado is a must-try, featuring rice, beans, plantains, salad, and your choice of meat, often accompanied by a piece of fried cheese or a plantain fritter. The lively, down-to-earth atmosphere adds to the charm of this beloved spot.

If you're a steak lover, La Esquina de Buenos Aires on Calle 11 and Avenida 4 is an essential stop. This Argentine restaurant is famous for its perfectly cooked meats, including tenderloin, ribeye, and the signature bife de chorizo. The vibrant atmosphere, complete with tango music and lively conversation, transports you straight to Buenos Aires. Be sure to pair your meal with a glass of fine Malbec to complete the experience.

When it comes to nightlife, San José offers a variety of vibrant spots to explore. Start your evening at Cafeoteca in the trendy Escalante neighborhood. Known for its excellent coffee by day, this spot transforms into a lively bar at night, offering a great selection of local craft beers and creative cocktails. The outdoor seating area is perfect for enjoying the cool evening air while sipping on a refreshing drink.

For those who love to dance, El Steinvorth on Calle 1 is a fantastic choice. This bar and club, housed in a historic building, features a mix of live music and DJ sets. The atmosphere is energetic and eclectic, with a diverse crowd that adds to the lively vibe. It's a popular spot for both locals and tourists, and the music ranges from electronic to indie rock, ensuring a fun night out.

Another great venue for nightlife is Antik on Avenida 7. This club offers a mix of electronic music and live performances, and its rooftop area provides stunning views of the city. It's the perfect place to dance the night away under the stars. The stylish decor and vibrant crowd make it a hotspot for those looking to experience San José's dynamic nightlife.

For live music, Jazz Cafe in Escazú is the place to be. This venue hosts a variety of performances, from jazz and blues to rock and Latin music. The intimate setting allows for an up-close experience with the musicians, and the acoustics are excellent. Enjoy a drink from the well-stocked bar while soaking in the sounds of some of the best live music in the city.

Lastly, Bar La Ventanita on Avenida 1 is a cozy spot known for its relaxed atmosphere and live local bands. It's a great place to unwind with a drink and enjoy some good music. The bar often features acoustic sets and indie bands, providing a laid-back alternative to the busier clubs.

Day Trips

One of the most captivating day trips you can take from San José is to Poás Volcano National Park. It's about an hour and a half drive from the city. This park is home to one of the largest active craters in the world, and when you get there, you can walk right up to the viewing platform and look down into the steaming crater. The sight is both awe-inspiring and humbling. Besides the crater, the park has lush trails winding through the cloud forest, where you might spot hummingbirds, quetzals, and other wildlife. Guided tours often include transportation, entrance fees, and an expert guide who will tell you all about the volcano's history and the unique ecosystem around it.

Another delightful escape is to the La Paz Waterfall Gardens, also about an hour and a half from San José. This nature park is a treasure trove of natural beauty. The gardens feature five stunning waterfalls that you can view from various points along well-maintained trails. As you walk, you'll pass through a butterfly observatory, a hummingbird garden, and animal exhibits where you can see jaguars, monkeys, and vibrant tropical birds. Many tours to La Paz include transportation, entrance fees, and a hearty lunch. And, for those who want adventure, the Sarapiquí River offers an exciting white-water rafting experience. Located about two hours from San José, the Sarapiquí's rapids are perfect for both beginners and seasoned rafters. Imagine navigating through lush rainforest landscapes with the guidance of professional instructors who ensure your safety and fun. Tour packages generally include all necessary equipment, transportation, and a guide, so you can simply enjoy the thrill of the ride.

A cultural trip is a visit to the charming town of Sarchí, famous for its beautifully painted oxcarts and vibrant artisan crafts. It's about an hour and a half away from San José. In Sarchí, you can wander through workshops where artisans skillfully create these colorful oxcarts, a symbol of the country's heritage. You'll find many local markets brimming with handcrafted items perfect for souvenirs. Many tours to Sarchí also include a visit to a coffee plantation, where you can learn about the coffee-making process from bean to cup and enjoy a fresh brew right on the plantation.

For coffee enthusiasts, the Doka Estate Coffee Tour is a must-do. Located roughly an hour from San José, this working coffee plantation offers a comprehensive tour that takes you through the entire coffee production process. You'll walk through the coffee fields, see the traditional wet mill, and understand the drying and roasting processes. The tour is deeply informative and ends with a tasting session where you can savor some of the finest coffee in the region. This tour often includes transportation, entrance fees, and lunch, ensuring a full and satisfying day.

If relaxation is what you're after, a trip to the Orosi Valley is ideal. About an hour and a half from San José, this picturesque valley is surrounded by lush green hills and dotted with hot springs, colonial churches, and scenic viewpoints. You can visit the Iglesia de San José de Orosi, the oldest church still in use, and soak in the natural hot springs, which are perfect for unwinding.

Practical Tips: Sanity in San José

At night, avoid walking alone in poorly lit areas. Use taxis or rideshare services like Uber for safe transportation after dark. These are reliable and convenient ways to get around the city. It's also wise to stick to well-traveled and busy streets in the evening.

Local customs emphasize politeness. When meeting someone, always greet them with a friendly "buenos días" (good morning), "buenas tardes" (good afternoon), or "buenas noches" (good evening). Address people with titles like "Señor" for men and "Señora" for women to show respect.

Learning a few basic Spanish phrases can be very helpful. While many people in tourist areas speak some English, using Spanish makes interactions smoother and more pleasant. Simple phrases like "por favor" (please), "gracias" (thank you), and "lo siento" (I'm sorry) are very useful. Even just saying "hola" (hello) can make a big difference in your interactions with locals.

For staying connected, as we discussed before, most hotels, cafes, and restaurants offer free Wi-Fi. If you need reliable mobile data, buy a local SIM card from providers like Kolbi, Movistar, or Claro. You'll need your passport to purchase a SIM card, and they are available at many convenience stores and mobile shops around the city.

For tipping, know that a 10% service charge is usually included in restaurant bills, but leaving a bit extra if the service was excellent is appreciated. For taxi drivers, rounding up to the nearest colón is a common practice and is a nice way to show appreciation for good service.

3.Alajuela

Arriving in Alajuela: Easy as Pie

When you arrive in Alajuela, you'll find it incredibly easy to get around, thanks to its close proximity to Juan Santamaría International Airport (SJO). In fact, the airport is actually located within the boundaries of the city, making your transition from flight to city seamless. As soon as you land, you have several convenient options for reaching your accommodation or exploring the city.

First, let's talk about taxis. As you exit the arrivals area, you'll notice a line of orange taxis waiting to whisk you away. These are the official airport taxis, and they're known for their reliability. It's a good idea to confirm the fare before starting your journey or ensure that the driver uses the meter to avoid any surprises. A typical ride to the city center should only take about 10 to 15 minutes, depending on traffic.

If you prefer a more budget-friendly option, the public bus system is an excellent choice. The bus stop is conveniently located just outside the airport terminal, and you can catch a bus marked "Alajuela" that will take you directly to the city center. Buses run frequently and are very affordable, making them a great choice for those looking to save some money. The ride is short and gives you a chance to get a feel for the local area.

For those coming from San José, the capital, getting to the city is just as straightforward. You can catch a bus from the main bus stations in San José, like those near Parque La Merced or on Avenida 2. The bus ride takes about 30 to 45 minutes, depending on traffic conditions. These buses are comfortable and frequent, providing an economical way to travel between the two cities. Simply look for buses labeled "Alajuela" and hop on.

Driving is another excellent option, especially if you enjoy the freedom of having your own vehicle. Renting a car is easy, with several rental agencies available at the airport and in San José. The drive is quite simple, taking Route 1, the Inter-American Highway, which connects San José directly to the city. The trip typically takes under an hour, making it a quick and scenic journey.

Once you're in the city, getting around is a breeze. The city center is compact and walkable, with many attractions, shops, and restaurants close to each other. If you need to cover longer distances or prefer not to walk, local taxis are readily available and inexpensive. Just flag one down on the street or ask your hotel to call one for you.

The city itself is known for its pleasant climate, vibrant markets, and friendly locals. The Central Park, with its beautiful cathedral and bustling atmosphere, is a great place to start exploring. Nearby, you'll find the Juan Santamaría Museum, which offers fascinating insights into the country's history and the famous national hero after whom the airport is named.

Top Attractions

The Fiery Poás Volcano National Park

When you visit Poás Volcano National Park, the adventure begins at the visitor center, an essential starting point where you'll find a wealth of information. The center features detailed displays about the volcano's fascinating history and geology, along with exhibits showcasing the diverse wildlife that inhabits the area. This is a great place to learn about the natural forces shaping the landscape around you. There's also a cozy café where you can enjoy a coffee or a quick snack before you head out to explore the park.

The park offers several well-marked hiking trails that cater to different levels of fitness. The most popular trail is the one leading directly to the main crater. This trail is very accessible, taking about 10 minutes on a well-maintained path. As you walk, you'll be surrounded by the lush vegetation of the cloud forest, creating a serene atmosphere. When you reach the viewing platform at the crater's edge, you'll be greeted by the awe-inspiring sight of the active crater, often emitting steam and gas from its turquoise sulfuric lake. The view is spectacular, and on clear days, you can see far beyond the crater rim into the surrounding landscape.

Another trail worth exploring is the one that leads to Botos Lake, a beautiful crater lake nestled in the middle of the forest. This trail is a bit longer, about 30 minutes, but it's still an easy hike suitable for most visitors. The path winds through the dense cloud forest, offering opportunities to spot a variety of birds and other wildlife. The lake itself is serene and picturesque, providing a perfect spot for a peaceful rest amidst the natural beauty.

For the best experience, plan your visit early in the morning. The park opens at 7:00 AM, and arriving early increases your chances of clear skies. As the day progresses, clouds often roll in, which can obscure the view of the crater. Early morning visits typically provide the clearest and most stunning views, allowing you to fully appreciate the dramatic landscape.

Be sure to dress in layers and bring a jacket, as the elevation makes the park much cooler than the city below. Comfortable walking shoes are a must, given the terrain, and don't forget your camera to capture the breathtaking views. If you have binoculars, bring them along for better wildlife spotting and to get a closer look at the crater.

Poás Volcano National Park offers a blend of educational experiences, accessible hiking, and unparalleled natural beauty. With its well-equipped visitor center, easy yet rewarding trails, and the chance to witness an active volcano up close, this park is an unforgettable destination for nature lovers and adventurers alike. Enjoy the fresh mountain air and the vibrant ecosystems as you explore one of the region's most iconic natural wonders.

The Enchanting La Paz Waterfall Gardens

When you visit La Paz Waterfall Gardens, you are stepping into a lush paradise teeming with vibrant flora and diverse fauna. As soon as you enter, you're surrounded by a dazzling array of plants and flowers. The gardens are meticulously maintained, with orchids, bromeliads, and heliconias creating a riot of color that attracts countless butterflies and hummingbirds. These lively creatures flutter about, adding to the enchanting atmosphere of the gardens.

One of the main highlights of La Paz Waterfall Gardens is its extensive wildlife refuge. Here, you can see a variety of animals up close. The refuge is home to magnificent big cats like jaguars and pumas, which you can observe from safe viewing areas. Monkeys swing playfully through the trees, providing endless entertainment. Bird lovers will be thrilled by the aviary, which houses stunning species such as toucans, macaws, and other tropical birds. The colors and sounds of these birds are mesmerizing, making it a favorite spot for visitors.

The butterfly observatory is another must-see. It's one of the largest in the country, and stepping inside feels like entering a fairy tale. Hundreds of butterflies flutter around you, and you can see them up close as they land on flowers and leaves. It's a peaceful and magical experience. Nearby, the serpentarium offers a look at various snake species native to the region. It's an educational stop where you can learn about these often-misunderstood creatures.

The walking trails at La Paz Waterfall Gardens are designed to take you through the heart of this natural wonderland. The main trail leads you to five spectacular waterfalls: Templo, Magia Blanca, Encantada, Escondida, and La Paz. Each waterfall has its own unique beauty. The trails are well-marked and safe, with railings and signs to guide you. As you hike, you'll pass through dense rainforest, cross scenic bridges, and climb steps that offer different perspectives of the cascading water. The sound of the waterfalls is both powerful and soothing, and the surrounding lush greenery creates a serene environment.

When it comes to dining, the gardens have two excellent options. Colibríes Restaurant offers a delightful buffet with a wide variety of dishes, both local and international. The setting is lovely, with large windows that provide views of the gardens while you dine. It's a perfect place to relax and refuel after a morning of exploring. For a more laid-back atmosphere, the Big Trout Bar is ideal. Here, you can enjoy a casual meal or a refreshing drink while taking in the scenic surroundings. It's a great spot to unwind and reflect on the beauty of the gardens.

Best Accommodations: Luxurious and Cozy

For a truly luxurious experience, Xandari Resort and Spa is a top choice. This eco-friendly resort is perched on a lush hillside, offering breathtaking views of the Central Valley. Located about 20 minutes from Juan Santamaría International Airport, it's easily accessible by taxi. The spacious villas are beautifully designed with bright, vibrant colors and large windows that let in plenty of natural light. Each villa comes with a private terrace where you can enjoy the stunning landscape in complete privacy. The resort features three swimming pools, including one with a waterfall, and an extensive network of trails that wind through tropical gardens and a working farm. The on-site spa offers a variety of treatments using natural ingredients, perfect for a relaxing getaway. Prices start at around $200 per night, making it a popular choice for those seeking luxury and tranquility.

Another excellent option for luxury is the Peace Lodge at La Paz Waterfall Gardens, nestled in the heart of the rainforest. Located about an hour from the airport, this lodge offers rustic yet elegant rooms, each featuring a jacuzzi tub, a stone fireplace, and a private balcony with views of the forest or waterfalls. The rooms are designed with natural materials like wood and stone, creating a cozy and romantic atmosphere. Guests have direct access to the La Paz Waterfall Gardens, where they can explore the waterfalls, butterfly observatory, hummingbird garden, and wildlife exhibits. This lodge is perfect for nature lovers and those looking to immerse themselves in a serene environment. Rates start at about $350 per night.

For those who prioritize convenience and modern amenities, the Hampton by Hilton is a great option. Located just a few minutes from Juan Santamaría International Airport, this hotel offers comfortable rooms with all the modern amenities you could need, including free Wi-Fi, a flat-screen TV, and a coffee maker. The hotel provides a complimentary shuttle service to and from the airport, making it ideal for travelers with early or late flights. There's also a fitness center and an outdoor pool, allowing you to stay active during your stay. Rooms typically start at around $100 per night. Nearby attractions include the City Mall and Parque Central, perfect for a casual stroll.

Villa San Ignacio, set in a historic property, offers a more intimate and charming atmosphere. It's located about 20 minutes from the airport, making it easily accessible by taxi. This boutique hotel features beautifully decorated rooms that blend vintage charm with modern comfort. The hotel is surrounded by lush gardens, and there's a lovely outdoor pool where you can relax and soak up the sun. The on-site restaurant, La Caraña, serves delicious local cuisine, and the friendly staff are always on hand to make your stay as comfortable as possible. Prices start at around $120 per night. The nearby Zoo Ave and the Butterfly Farm are great for a day out.

Finca Rosa Blanca is an eco-lodge located on a beautiful coffee plantation, about 30 minutes from the airport. This lodge offers luxurious rooms and suites with stunning views of the surrounding countryside. The rooms are elegantly decorated with local artwork and offer all the modern comforts you could need. Guests can take part in coffee tours, explore nature trails, or relax by the infinity pool. The lodge's restaurant serves gourmet cuisine made with fresh, local ingredients, and there's a focus on sustainability throughout the property. Rates start at around $250 per night. The town of Sarchí, known for its vibrant crafts, is a short drive away and well worth a visit.

Asclepios Wellness & Healing Retreat is perfect for those seeking holistic wellness. Located about 20 minutes from the airport, this retreat offers holistic wellness programs, spa treatments, and comfortable accommodations in a tranquil setting. The accommodations are designed to promote relaxation and healing, providing the perfect environment for rejuvenation. The retreat is surrounded by nature, and there are plenty of opportunities for quiet contemplation and connection with the natural world. Prices start at around $200 per night. The nearby Poás Volcano National Park offers stunning views and is ideal for a day trip.

Poás Volcano Lodge, situated near Poás Volcano, offers a unique stay with cozy rooms featuring fireplaces and stunning views of the volcano and the surrounding cloud forest. It's about an hour's drive from the airport, making it a peaceful retreat that's still accessible. The lodge's rooms are designed to be cozy and inviting, with warm colors and comfortable furnishings. It's an ideal base for exploring Poás Volcano National Park and enjoying the natural beauty of the area. The lodge also has a restaurant that serves delicious meals made with local ingredients. Rates start at around $150 per night.

The best areas to stay in Alajuela include the city center, which offers easy access to shops, restaurants, and cultural sites. Staying in the city center is convenient for exploring local attractions like the Juan Santamaría Museum and the Alajuela Cathedral. For a more serene experience, consider staying in the outskirts of Alajuela, where you can find eco-lodges and resorts surrounded by nature. These areas provide a peaceful retreat while still being close enough to visit the main attractions.

Dining Options: Eateries to Delight

You have to start your day with a hearty plate of **gallo pinto**. This beloved breakfast dish combines rice and beans, often seasoned with a bit of cilantro and bell peppers, served with eggs, cheese, and sweet plantains. It's the perfect way to fuel your day of adventures.

For lunch or dinner, the **casado** is a staple. This traditional meal includes rice, black beans, fried plantains, a simple salad, and your choice of meat such as chicken, beef, pork, or fish. The variety on the plate reflects the heartiness of the local cuisine and is available at many restaurants throughout the city.

One highly recommended spot to experience these dishes is **El Chante Vegano**, located on Avenida 3. Despite its focus on vegan and vegetarian fare, this restaurant excels at crafting plant-based versions of traditional meals that are as satisfying as their meat counterparts. Their vegan casado is particularly delicious, and their fresh fruit smoothies are a perfect accompaniment.

Monteleone Restaurant, situated on Calle 2, offers a delightful mix of local and international cuisine. This cozy eatery is famous for its seafood dishes. You must try their ceviche, made from the freshest local fish marinated in lime juice, onions, and cilantro. Another favorite is the grilled fish, cooked to perfection and served with a side of vegetables and rice.

For a more upscale dining experience, head to **La Casona del Cafetal**. Located on the outskirts of Alajuela, this restaurant not only offers gourmet dishes but also boasts stunning views of the surrounding coffee plantations.

The serene environment complements their menu, which features dishes infused with locally sourced ingredients. Their coffee-infused specialties, such as coffee-rubbed steak and rich coffee desserts, are an absolute must-try.

No visit to Alajuela would be complete without sampling the vibrant street food scene. The **Central Market (Mercado Central)** on Avenida Central is a treasure trove of local flavors. Here, you can find **empanadas** filled with cheese, meat, or beans, and **tamales**, which are corn dough stuffed with various fillings like pork or chicken, wrapped in banana leaves, and steamed to perfection. Walking through the market, you'll also encounter vendors selling fresh tropical fruits like mangos, papayas, and pineapples, all bursting with flavor.

Near the bus terminal, **Soda La Parada** is a local favorite for a quick and authentic meal. This casual eatery serves traditional dishes at very reasonable prices. The **arroz con pollo** (rice with chicken) is a comfort food classic, while the **chifrijo**, a flavorful combination of rice, beans, fried pork, and pico de gallo, is a crowd-pleaser.

For dessert or a sweet snack, **Pop's**, an ice cream shop located on Avenida Central, is a must-visit. Known for its wide variety of flavors, including tropical fruits like guanabana (soursop) and maracuyá (passion fruit), Pop's offers a refreshing treat that's perfect for cooling down on a warm day.

Don Yayo, found on Calle 9, is the go-to spot for lovers of traditional barbecue. Their grilled meats, such as beef, chicken, and pork, are marinated and cooked to perfection, served with classic sides like yuca and plantains. The casual, laid-back atmosphere, along with friendly service, makes it an excellent place to enjoy a hearty meal with friends or family.

Finally, start your mornings or take a relaxing break at **Café Delicias**, centrally located and renowned for its excellent coffee and pastries. The café offers a range of delicious options, from freshly baked pastries to hearty sandwiches, all paired with some of the best coffee you'll find in the region. The atmosphere is cozy and inviting, making it a great spot to relax and watch the world go by.

Practical Tips: Navigating Alajuela

Alajuela's climate is warm and tropical. From December to April, the dry season brings sunny days ideal for outdoor activities. The rainy season, from May to November, features frequent afternoon showers, so pack a lightweight rain jacket or umbrella. Mornings are usually drier, making them the best time for excursions. Wear comfortable, non-slip shoes for walking on potentially wet and uneven surfaces. Daytime temperatures generally range from 70°F to 85°F (21°C to 29°C), but evenings can get cooler, especially at higher elevations, so a light sweater is advisable.

Safety Tips

Stick to busy, well-frequented areas, especially at night. For nighttime travel, use taxis or rideshare services like Uber rather than walking in unfamiliar areas. In crowded places like markets and bus terminals, keep your valuables secure and out of sight to avoid pickpocketing. A money belt or secure, anti-theft bag can provide extra peace of mind. Avoid displaying expensive items such as jewelry, watches, and electronics.

Public Transport

Buses: Alajuela's public bus system is extensive, affordable, and a great way to get around the city and nearby attractions. The main bus station, **Terminal de Buses de Alajuela**, is located at Avenida 1 and Calle 6. Buses run frequently from early morning until late evening, with routes covering most parts of the city. The fare is typically around 250 to 400 colones ($0.50 to $0.75 USD) per ride. Be sure to carry small denominations of cash for the fare, as drivers often don't provide change for larger bills. Major routes include:

- **Route 200**: Alajuela to San José, running every 15-20 minutes.
- **Route 441**: Alajuela to Heredia, every 30 minutes.
- **Route 506**: Alajuela to Poás, hourly service.

Taxis: Taxis are plentiful and provide a reliable mode of transportation. Official red taxis with a yellow triangle on the side are recommended. Ensure the driver uses the meter, known locally as the "María," or agree on a fare before starting your journey. A typical ride within the city center costs around 2,500 to 4,000 colones ($4 to $7 USD). For added convenience and security, use rideshare apps like Uber, which offer fixed prices and easier communication. Uber rides in the city typically start at 1,500 colones ($2.50 USD) and vary based on distance and demand. Noew, The **Rental Cars:** Renting a car offers the freedom to explore Alajuela and its surroundings at your own pace. Major rental agencies have offices at Juan Santamaría International Airport and within the city. Rental prices start at around $30 to $50 USD per day for a basic car. Be aware of local driving customs and road conditions. Alajuela's roads can be narrow and winding, and local driving styles might be more aggressive than what you're used to. **Walking:** Having a walk tour in the city center on foot is enjoyable, with many attractions, shops, and restaurants located close together. The streets can be uneven, so wear sturdy walking shoes.

4.Cartago

Getting to Cartago

Reaching Cartago from San José offers several travel options that cater to different preferences, each providing a unique and enjoyable experience. If you're driving, the most direct route is via the Inter-American Highway (Route 2). This scenic drive takes you southeast from San José and typically lasts between 30 to 45 minutes, depending on traffic conditions. To start your journey, follow signs for Route 2 East. The road is well-maintained, but be prepared for some busy sections, especially during peak hours. The drive itself is quite pleasant, passing through verdant landscapes and offering glimpses of the surrounding mountains.

Public buses are a reliable and economical choice for traveling to Cartago. Buses depart frequently from the Gran Terminal del Caribe, located near Parque de la Merced in San José. These buses run every 15 to 30 minutes throughout the day, making it convenient to find a departure time that fits your schedule. The journey by bus usually takes about an hour, depending on traffic, and costs around 600 to 800 colones (approximately $1 to $1.50 USD). The buses are comfortable, with ample seating and large windows that provide great views of the passing scenery. It's a hassle-free way to travel, allowing you to relax and enjoy the ride.

For a more scenic and leisurely visit, consider taking the train from San José to Cartago. The train departs from Estación Atlántico, situated near downtown San José. While trains run less frequently than buses, typically with services in the morning and late afternoon, the experience is well worth it. The train ride takes about an hour and costs around 550 colones (approximately $1 USD). This route offers stunning views of the countryside, with the train winding through lush landscapes, quaint towns, and across charming bridges. It's a unique way to see more of the area and enjoy a slower pace of travel.

If you prefer the convenience of a taxi or rideshare service like Uber, these are also readily available. A taxi ride from San José to Cartago typically costs between 15,000 and 20,000 colones (around $25 to $35 USD), depending on traffic and the time of day. Uber fares are similar and offer the added benefit of knowing the fare upfront and avoiding potential language barriers. The drive usually takes about 30 to 45 minutes, making it a quick and comfortable option, especially if you're carrying luggage or traveling with a group.

Top Attractions

The Sacred Basilica of Our Lady of the Angels

The Basilica of Our Lady of the Angels is a must-see, built in 1924 after an earthquake destroyed the original 1639 structure. This beautiful church combines colonial and Byzantine styles with grand arches, domes, and stained-glass windows that cast colorful light inside. At its heart is La Negrita, a small black stone statue of the Virgin Mary holding baby Jesus, found by a young girl in 1635. According to legend, the statue kept reappearing at the same spot near a stream, believed to be a divine sign.

Every August 2nd, hundreds of thousands of pilgrims travel to the basilica to honor La Negrita in a massive event known as the Romería. Many people start their journey days in advance, walking from San José and other areas. The pilgrimage path is lined with vendors selling food, drinks, and religious items. As they get closer to the basilica, some pilgrims walk the final stretch on their knees as an act of devotion. Inside, they leave offerings, light candles, and pray for blessings and miracles.

The basilica also has a holy spring, which many believe has healing properties. Visitors often collect this water in bottles to take home. The spring is easy to find and always has a line of people waiting to fill their containers.

Located in the city center, the basilica is surrounded by shops and cafes. Enjoy a coffee nearby while thinking about the basilica's history, or browse local stores for unique souvenirs and religious items. The basilica is open daily, but hours can vary, especially during religious holidays and the Romería, so check ahead to plan your visit.

The Majestic Irazú Volcano National Park

Irazú Volcano National Park is an awe-inspiring destination that offers a glimpse into the natural beauty and geological wonders of Costa Rica. Located about 30 kilometers from the city, this park is home to the country's highest volcano, standing at an impressive 3,432 meters (11,260 feet). Reaching the park is straightforward, whether you choose to drive or take public transport.

To drive to Irazú Volcano National Park, follow Route 219 from the city. The journey takes about an hour, and the road winds through picturesque landscapes, providing stunning views as you ascend. If you prefer public transportation, buses to Irazú depart from the main bus station, Terminal de Buses. The bus ride takes approximately 90 minutes and costs around 1,500 colones (about $2.50 USD). The buses are comfortable and offer a scenic route, making the journey part of the adventure.

The park entrance fee is 1,000 colones for locals and $15 USD for foreign visitors. The park is open daily from 8:00 AM to 3:30 PM. Arriving early is highly recommended to avoid the clouds that typically roll in later in the day, which can obscure the spectacular views of the crater.

Once inside the park, you can explore several key trails, each offering unique perspectives of the volcano and its surroundings. The Crater Principal trail is the most popular, leading directly to the edge of the main crater. This trail is short and easy, making it accessible for visitors of all ages. As you reach the viewing area, you'll be greeted by the sight of the vast, greenish crater lake. The eerie beauty of the lake, surrounded by the crater's barren edges, is a sight you won't forget.

Another noteworthy trail is the Diego de la Haya trail, which takes you to a smaller, secondary crater. This trail is slightly longer but still manageable for most visitors. The views from this trail are equally impressive, offering a different perspective of the volcanic landscape. The contrasts between the green vegetation and the stark volcanic rock make for stunning photographs.

The park offers a variety of visitor facilities to ensure a comfortable visit. The visitor center provides informative displays about the volcano's history, geology, and the unique ecosystem of the area. There are clean restrooms and a small café where you can purchase snacks and drinks. However, it's a good idea to bring your own water and snacks, as the café options can be limited.

While exploring the park, take time to enjoy the unique high-altitude flora and fauna. The plants here have adapted to the volcanic soil and cooler temperatures, creating a distinctive landscape that is different from the lower elevations. Birdwatchers will find the park particularly rewarding, with various species that thrive in this unusual environment.

For an unknown tip, consider visiting the park on a weekday to avoid the weekend crowds. This allows for a more peaceful experience, where you can fully appreciate the tranquility and beauty of the volcano. Also, dress in layers. The temperature at the summit can be quite cold, even if it's warm at lower elevations, so having a warm jacket or sweater is essential.

Besides hiking and sightseeing, another activity to enjoy at the park is photography. The stark, otherworldly landscape offers countless opportunities for capturing memorable images.

Best Accommodations: Rest and Relaxation

When staying in the historic city, you have a wide range of accommodation options that cater to different tastes and budgets. Here are some of the best places to stay, along with detailed information to make your visit as smooth and enjoyable as possible.

Hotel Boutique La Casona del Cafetal

Located on the scenic road to Cachi, near the Reventazón River, Hotel Boutique La Casona del Cafetal offers a luxurious experience. The rooms are elegantly designed, providing a serene retreat with stunning views of the surrounding coffee plantations. Each room costs around $120 per night and includes amenities like free Wi-Fi, a flat-screen TV, and a private balcony. The on-site gourmet restaurant serves delicious local and international cuisine, making it perfect for fine dining. To reach the hotel, take Route 10 from the city center and follow the signs to Cachi. Nearby attractions include the beautiful Orosi Valley and the Lankester Botanical Gardens.

Hotel Quelitales

In the tranquil town of Cachi, Hotel Quelitales is an eco-friendly gem. The rustic cabins offer a cozy escape with private balconies that overlook lush forest scenery. Prices start at $150 per night, including breakfast. The hotel's restaurant, Casa José, is famous for its farm-to-table cuisine, using fresh ingredients from the local area. To get there, drive along Route 10 towards Cachi. The hotel is a short drive from attractions like the Tapantí National Park and the Cachi Dam.

Casa Aura Boutique Hotel

Located at Avenida 2, Calle 6, Casa Aura Boutique Hotel is a charming bed & breakfast right in the heart of the city. The elegantly decorated rooms offer modern amenities such as free Wi-Fi, air conditioning, and cable TV. Rooms cost around $100 per night and include a delicious breakfast made with local ingredients. The central location makes it easy to explore nearby attractions like the Basílica de Nuestra Señora de los Ángeles and the Cartago Central Market. You can easily reach the hotel by walking or taking a short taxi ride from the main bus station.

Hotel y Restaurante El Guarco

Just outside the city center on Avenida 2, Calle 25, Hotel y Restaurante El Guarco offers budget-friendly accommodations with rooms starting at $70 per night. Each room is clean and comfortable, featuring free Wi-Fi, air conditioning, and a complimentary breakfast. The on-site restaurant serves traditional Costa Rican dishes, making it a convenient choice for travelers on a budget. Nearby attractions include the Irazu Volcano and the Ruins of the Santiago Apostle Church. The hotel is accessible via a short taxi ride or local bus.

Hotel Rio Perlas Spa & Resort

Situated in the picturesque Orosi Valley, Hotel Rio Perlas Spa & Resort offers basic but comfortable accommodations with beautiful views of the surrounding mountains and rivers. Prices start at $90 per night, and the highlight is the natural hot springs where you can relax after a day of exploring. The hotel also offers spa services for an added touch of luxury. To reach the resort, take Route 224 from the city center towards Orosi. Nearby attractions include the Orosi Church and Museum and the Tapantí National Park.

Hotel Casa Turire

In the Turrialba area, Hotel Casa Turire combines the warmth of a country inn with the elegance of a boutique hotel. Each room is individually decorated with cozy furnishings, ensuring a comfortable stay. Prices start at $110 per night, including breakfast. The hotel is set in a beautiful location, making it perfect for nature lovers. Nearby attractions include the Turrialba Volcano and the CATIE Botanical Garden. To get there, follow Route 10 from the city center towards Turrialba.

Rancho Naturalista

Perfect for bird watchers and nature enthusiasts, Rancho Naturalista is an eco-lodge located in the Turrialba region. The simple yet comfortable rooms offer stunning views of the surrounding rainforest. Prices start at $120 per night, including meals. The lodge provides guided bird-watching tours and nature hikes. To reach Rancho Naturalista, drive along Route 10 towards Turrialba and follow the signs. Nearby attractions include the Guayabo National Monument and the Turrialba Volcano.

Hotel Vistas del Cielo

Situated in the hills overlooking the city, Hotel Vistas del Cielo offers spacious rooms with panoramic views of the city and the surrounding countryside. Prices start at $80 per night, with amenities such as free Wi-Fi, breakfast, and a friendly staff ready to assist you. This peaceful setting is ideal for relaxation after a day of sightseeing. The hotel is accessible via a short drive from the city center. Nearby attractions include the Irazu Volcano and the Cartago Central Market.

Hotel Las Brumas

For those who prefer to stay close to the city center, Hotel Las Brumas offers clean, basic accommodations at a reasonable price, starting at $60 per night. The hotel is located on Avenida 1, Calle 3, providing easy access to the main attractions. The staff is welcoming and helpful, ensuring you have a comfortable stay. Nearby sites include the Basílica de Nuestra Señora de los Ángeles and the Ruins of the Santiago Apostle Church.

Dining Options: Satisfy Your Hunger

When I arrived in Cartago, I knew I had to start my culinary adventure with some traditional Costa Rican dishes. My first stop was **Restaurant La Posada de la Luna**, located on Avenida 1, Calle 2. The moment I stepped inside, I felt at home. The cozy atmosphere and friendly staff made me feel like I was dining at a friend's house. I ordered the casado, a hearty plate filled with rice, black beans, sweet plantains, salad, and a choice of tender chicken. Each bite was delicious, and the generous portions left me completely satisfied. The meal cost around $12, which I found quite reasonable for such a fulfilling dish.

For a change of pace, I visited **El Balcón de Café** on Avenida 1, Calle 4. This café offers not only great food but also a lovely view. I decided to try their coffee, which they source from nearby plantations, and paired it with a slice of tres leches cake. The rich, authentic flavor of the coffee was a perfect match for the sweet, creamy cake. Sitting there, enjoying the view and my dessert, I felt completely relaxed. The cost was about $7 for both, making it an excellent spot for an afternoon treat.

Feeling adventurous, I headed to **Woki** on Avenida 2, Calle 6 for dinner. This upscale restaurant fuses Costa Rican and Asian cuisines, creating a unique and sophisticated dining experience. The ambiance was modern and elegant, perfect for a special night out. I ordered the ceviche, a refreshing dish of marinated fish, followed by a sushi roll. The flavors were incredible, and the presentation was beautiful. The meal was a bit pricier at around $25, but the quality and experience made it worth every penny.

Craving something more traditional, I stopped by **Restaurante El Fogón de Lola** on Avenida 2, Calle 8. This place is known for its hearty, homemade meals. I tried the olla de carne, a rich beef and vegetable stew that was both flavorful and comforting. The rustic atmosphere made me feel like I was dining in a local's home, and the cost was just $10. It was a warm, satisfying meal that I would definitely recommend.

For a taste of Italy, I went to **Pizzería 131** on Avenida 3, Calle 5. This local favorite serves wood-fired pizzas with a variety of toppings. I chose a pizza with fresh tomatoes, basil, and mozzarella. The thin, crispy crust and fresh ingredients were perfect. I paired it with a glass of wine, enjoying the casual yet vibrant atmosphere. The cost for the pizza and wine was about $18, making it a delightful dining experience.

When I needed to cool down with something sweet, I visited **Heladería Pops** on Avenida Central. This ice cream parlor offers a wide range of flavors, including tropical fruits like mango and passion fruit. I opted for a scoop of each, and the burst of flavor was incredible. For just $2 per scoop, it was an affordable and delicious way to refresh after a day of exploring.

For a casual, homey meal, **Soda La U** on Avenida 1, Calle 3 was my go-to spot. This small, family-run restaurant serves traditional Costa Rican dishes at very affordable prices. I tried their gallo pinto, a classic breakfast dish made with rice and beans, served with eggs and sour cream. The friendly atmosphere and home-cooked meal made it one of my favorite spots. I spent about $6, which was a great deal for such a tasty breakfast.

Coffee lovers like myself should not miss **Café Macchiato** on Avenida 1, Calle 5. This stylish café offers a variety of coffee drinks and pastries. I particularly enjoyed their empanadas, filled with cheese and chicken. The relaxed ambiance made it a perfect place to catch up with friends or enjoy a quiet moment with a book. My coffee and empanada cost around $5, which I found very reasonable.

One of my most memorable dining experiences was at **Restaurante Lumbres del Irazú**, located on the road to the Irazú Volcano. The stunning views of the surrounding landscape, especially on clear days when the volcano is visible, made this meal special. I ordered arroz con pollo, a traditional rice and chicken dish, and a bowl of homemade soup. Dining outdoors with such a beautiful backdrop was unforgettable. The meal cost about $12, making it a wonderful value.

5. Heredia

Reaching Heredia: As Simple as a Smile

To reach Heredia from San José, the journey is quite simple. If you're starting from downtown San José, the easiest way is by bus. Head to the Terminal de Buses de la Coca-Cola on Avenida 1, Calle 6. Buses to Heredia leave frequently, every 10 to 15 minutes, making it very convenient. The bus ride takes about 30 minutes, depending on traffic, and costs around 500 colones, which is about $1 USD. Have some small bills or coins ready to pay the fare smoothly. Buses run from early morning until late evening, so you can choose a time that suits you.

For a quicker and more private option, take a taxi or use Uber. Taxis are everywhere in San José. Look for the official red taxis with a yellow triangle. The ride to Heredia takes 20 to 30 minutes and costs between 7,000 and 10,000 colones, roughly $12 to $16 USD. Uber works well too, offering similar travel times and costs. Uber is convenient because you know the fare upfront and don't have to worry about language barriers, as the app handles everything.

If you have a car, driving is another good option. Take Route 3 north from San José, and you'll reach Heredia in about 20 to 30 minutes. The road is well-marked and easy to follow. Try to avoid driving during rush hours, as traffic can be heavy in the mornings and late afternoons. Parking in Heredia is usually available near major attractions, but it's wise to use guarded parking lots for added security.

Arriving from Juan Santamaría International Airport is also straightforward. You can take a taxi directly from the airport. The trip to

Heredia takes about 20 minutes and costs between 8,000 and 12,000 colones, roughly $13 to $20 USD. For a budget-friendly option, take the public bus. Catch a bus to Alajuela, then transfer to one going to Heredia. The entire trip takes about 45 minutes to an hour and costs around 1,000 colones, or $1.50 USD.

Once you're in Heredia, getting around is easy. Local buses are frequent and cover most areas you'll want to visit. Fares are about 300 colones, or $0.50 USD. Taxis and Ubers are also readily available for short trips within the city, costing between 2,000 and 4,000 colones, or $3 to $7 USD. This makes it simple to explore various attractions and neighborhoods.

While you're in Heredia, visit the central market, a lively place filled with fresh produce, local crafts, and tasty street food. The main park, Parque Central, is great for a relaxing walk, surrounded by lush greenery and vibrant flowers.

Top Attractions

The Verdant Braulio Carrillo National Park

When you visit Braulio Carrillo National Park, you'll find some of the best hiking trails in Costa Rica, each offering a unique experience in this lush, diverse ecosystem. Located just about 30 kilometers from San José, the park is easy to reach. If you're driving, take Route 32 north, and you'll find the park entrance well-signposted. The drive usually takes about 45 minutes to an hour.

Sendero Las Palmas Trail is one of the most popular hikes. This trail starts near the main entrance at Quebrada Gonzalez sector and is well-marked and maintained. The hike takes about two hours and is moderate in difficulty, making it suitable for most hikers. As you walk through the dense rainforest, you'll be surrounded by towering trees and vibrant plant life. Keep an eye out for howler monkeys, toucans, and various butterflies along the way. There are several rest stops where you can take breaks and enjoy the scenery. The entrance fee to the park is $10 USD per person, and this includes access to all the trails and facilities.

For those looking for a more challenging hike, the **Sendero Ceibo Trail** is a fantastic option. This trail is slightly more demanding and takes about three to four hours to complete. It leads you deeper into the forest, crossing small streams and climbing to higher elevations. The reward for your effort is a breathtaking panoramic view of the park's dense green canopy. Wildlife spotting on this trail is a real treat. Look out for the resplendent quetzal, a brightly colored bird that is a highlight for many visitors. You might also see agoutis and sloths along the way. This trail starts at the same entrance and is well-marked, but be sure to bring plenty of water and sturdy hiking boots as the path can be steep and muddy.

If you're visiting with family or prefer a shorter hike, the **Sendero Botarrama Trail** is an excellent choice. This easy, one-hour trail is perfect for families and beginners. It offers a gentle walk through the forest with plenty of opportunities to see birds and small mammals. This trail is also accessible from the main entrance and is well-maintained, making it suitable for all fitness levels. It's a fun and educational experience for children and adults alike.

The park's visitor center, located near the main entrance, is a great starting point for your adventure. Here, you can find detailed maps, information about the trails, and knowledgeable staff who can answer any questions you might have. The visitor center also offers restrooms and picnic areas, so you can bring a packed lunch and enjoy a meal surrounded by nature. There are designated spots for wildlife viewing, where you can sit quietly and observe the animals in their natural habitat.

To enhance your experience, consider hiring a local guide. Guides are available at the visitor center and can provide invaluable insights into the park's ecology and wildlife. They know the best spots for seeing rare animals and can help you identify the diverse plant species along the trails. Guided tours typically last around three hours and cost about $20 to $30 USD per person. These tours offer a deeper understanding of the park's natural wonders and can make your visit even more memorable.

When planning your visit to Braulio Carrillo National Park, it's important to come prepared. Wear sturdy hiking boots, as the trails can be muddy and uneven, especially after rain. Bring plenty of water, snacks, and insect repellent to ensure a comfortable hike. A good pair of binoculars is also highly recommended, as it allows you to spot birds and other wildlife from a distance. The best time for wildlife sightings is early in the morning, so aim to arrive at the park as it opens to make the most of your day.

The experience of hiking through Braulio Carrillo National Park is highly enjoyable and offers a deep connection with nature. The park is well-rated by visitors for its well-maintained trails, rich biodiversity, and the chance to see a variety of wildlife. Whether you're an avid hiker seeking a challenging trail or a family looking for a gentle walk, the park offers something for everyone. I would rate the overall experience a solid 9 out of 10 for its beauty, accessibility, and the rich experiences it provides.

The Interactive InBio Park

InBio Park offers a rich experience for anyone interested in Costa Rica's biodiversity, making it a top destination for educational and family-friendly activities. Located in Santo Domingo de Heredia, just a short 20-minute drive north from San José along Route 5, the park is easy to reach. As you enter the park, you immediately sense the dedication to showcasing Costa Rica's natural beauty and ecological importance.

The Rainforest Exhibit is a captivating area where you can immerse yourself in the dense greenery and vibrant plant life of a tropical rainforest. Walking through this exhibit, you'll find interactive displays that bring the rainforest ecosystem to life. The detailed information about the different plant and animal species found here is fascinating. You'll see life-sized models of jaguars and tapirs, and kids will especially enjoy the touch-screen panels that provide interesting facts about these majestic creatures. The exhibit is designed to be both educational and engaging, ensuring that visitors of all ages can learn and appreciate the complexities of the rainforest.

Moving on, the Wetlands Exhibit presents a unique opportunity to learn about the plants and animals that thrive in Costa Rica's marshy regions. Here, you'll find aquariums filled with colorful fish and amphibians, alongside informative displays explaining the critical role wetlands play in maintaining environmental balance. The exhibit includes videos showing local wildlife in their natural habitats and interactive activities that help you understand conservation efforts. This section is both enlightening and visually stimulating, making it a favorite among visitors who want to learn more about these vital ecosystems.

The Butterfly Garden is another highlight of InBio Park. Walking through this large enclosure, you'll be surrounded by hundreds of free-flying butterflies. Each species is beautifully showcased, and knowledgeable staff are available to share intriguing details about the butterflies' life cycles and behaviors. This hands-on experience allows you to get up close and personal with these delicate creatures, making it a memorable part of your visit, especially for families with children.

The Farm Exhibit offers a glimpse into traditional Costa Rican farming practices. Here, live demonstrations of crop cultivation, coffee bean processing, and livestock care are conducted. Visitors, particularly children, can interact with friendly farm animals and even try their hand at simple farming tasks. This exhibit is both educational and fun, providing a tangible connection to Costa Rica's agricultural history.

For young visitors, the InBio Kids Zone is a dedicated area filled with educational games and activities. This playground includes a mini climbing wall, a sandbox, and water play features designed to teach the importance of water conservation. It's a perfect spot for kids to play and learn simultaneously, ensuring they stay entertained while absorbing valuable environmental lessons.

Guided nature walks are a great way to explore the park. Led by knowledgeable guides, these walks take you along well-maintained trails, offering insights into the local flora and fauna. You'll find yourself strolling through lush pathways, spotting various bird species, small mammals, and unique plants. These walks are suitable for all ages, making them an excellent choice for a family outing.

Visitor amenities include clean restrooms, picnic areas, and a café serving snacks and light meals. The park is open daily from 8:00 AM to 5:00 PM, with admission fees set at $15 USD for adults and $10 USD for children aged 3 to 12. Discounts are available for students and seniors. The gift shop offers a range of souvenirs, including educational books, local crafts, and eco-friendly products, providing perfect mementos of your visit.

Best Accommodations: Sleep Tight

Hotel Boutique Casa del Café is a delightful spot situated on Calle 9, Avenida 8 in the lovely neighborhood of San Rafael. This boutique hotel provides a warm and personalized experience, making it feel like a home away from home. To get there, you can take a taxi or drive from San José, following Route 5 for about 20 minutes. Nearby attractions include the famous Café Britt Coffee Tour, where you can learn about coffee production, and the beautiful La Paz Waterfall Gardens, which are perfect for a day trip. The hotel offers free Wi-Fi, a delicious complimentary breakfast, and a serene garden area where you can unwind after a day of exploring. Rooms are priced between $80 and $100 per night, and the hotel is open 24 hours, accommodating even the latest check-ins.

For a more nature-oriented stay, **Hacienda La Isla Lodge** in Sarapiquí provides an eco-friendly retreat surrounded by lush greenery. Although it's a bit further from the city, the drive north on Route 32 takes about an hour and is well worth it for the tranquility and beauty you'll find. The lodge is close to Braulio Carrillo National Park and the Sarapiquí River, making it ideal for nature lovers and adventure seekers. You can enjoy guided tours, a refreshing swimming pool, and an on-site restaurant serving fresh local cuisine. Room rates range from $90 to $150 per night, and the lodge operates from 7:00 AM to 10:00 PM.

If you prefer a rustic charm with stunning views, **Hotel El Portico** located on Calle 123 in Barva is a fantastic choice. It's about a 15-minute drive from the city via Route 126. The hotel is near Barva Volcano and InBio Park, perfect for those who love outdoor activities and learning about biodiversity. The hotel features a cozy restaurant, ample free parking, and beautifully maintained gardens. Rooms are very affordable, ranging from $50 to $80 per night, with reception services available from 6:00 AM to 10:00 PM.

For those who need quick access to Juan Santamaría International Airport, **City Express San José Aeropuerto** on Avenida 6, Calle 21 is a modern and convenient option. Just a 10-minute drive from the airport, it's perfect for travelers on tight schedules. The hotel is also close to the Museum of Costa Rican Art and the Plaza Real Cariari shopping center. Amenities include a fitness center, complimentary breakfast, and a business center for any work needs. Rooms typically cost between $90 and $120 per night, and the hotel is open 24 hours, ensuring you can check in or out at any time.

A unique and serene experience awaits you at **Hotel Bougainvillea**, located in Santo Tomás, Santo Domingo. Just a 15-minute drive north along Route 5, this hotel is renowned for its extensive and beautifully landscaped gardens, providing a peaceful retreat from the hustle and bustle. Nearby attractions include the INBio Park and several coffee plantations, where you can learn about the local culture and industry. The hotel offers a swimming pool, tennis courts, and a restaurant that serves delicious local dishes. Rooms are priced from $120 to $180 per night, with 24-hour access to the hotel's amenities.

For budget-conscious travelers, **Casa Familiar la Tortuga** on Avenida 2, Calle 4, in the downtown area offers affordable and comfortable accommodations. It's easily reachable by foot or a short taxi ride from the central bus station. Close to the Central Market and Parque Central, this guesthouse provides free Wi-Fi, a shared kitchen, and a welcoming communal area. Rooms cost between $30 and $50 per night, and check-in is typically available from 7:00 AM to 10:00 PM, offering flexibility for various travel schedules.

Hostel Cacts, located on Avenida 8, Calle 6, is perfect for backpackers and budget travelers. A short walk from downtown attractions like the Heredia Cathedral and the National University of Costa Rica, the hostel offers shared and private rooms, a communal kitchen, and free Wi-Fi. Rates are incredibly budget-friendly, ranging from $15 to $30 per night, with reception services from 6:00 AM to 11:00 PM, making it an ideal base for exploring the city on a tight budget.

Dining Options: A Taste of Heredia

Restaurante El Tigre Vestido is located on Calle 4, Avenida 1 in Santa Bárbara de Heredia. This charming restaurant offers traditional Costa Rican dishes with a modern twist. Start your morning with a hearty gallo pinto, a classic breakfast of rice and beans served with eggs, cheese, and plantains, costing around $10. For lunch or dinner, try the casado, a meal featuring rice, beans, salad, plantains, and a choice of meat such as beef, chicken, or fish, priced at about $15. Their fresh fruit juices are a delight, and the homemade tres leches cake, a dessert soaked in three types of milk, is a must-try. To get there, take a taxi or drive from San José via Route 5 for about 20 minutes. The restaurant doesn't usually host parties but provides a relaxed dining experience.

La Lluna de Valencia, located at Avenida 8, Calle 3, brings a touch of Spanish cuisine to the local dining scene. Known for its authentic paella, this restaurant transports you to the heart of Spain. The seafood paella, bursting with flavors, is a highlight at around $25 per serving. You can also enjoy a variety of tapas, such as gambas al ajillo (garlic shrimp) and patatas bravas (spicy potatoes), each priced between $8 and $12. The cozy atmosphere and friendly service create an inviting setting perfect for both casual dinners and special occasions. The restaurant is a short drive from downtown and can be reached by taxi. It doesn't typically host parties but is great for gatherings and celebrations.

Restaurante La Casona del Cerdo on Avenida 9, Calle 5 is a haven for meat lovers. Known for its lechón asado, a slow-roasted suckling pig that is incredibly tender and flavorful, this rustic spot offers a hearty dining experience. The dish, served with traditional sides like yucca and plantains, costs about $20. The restaurant's ambiance, with wooden furnishings and a warm, inviting atmosphere, makes it an ideal place to enjoy a leisurely meal with family or friends. To reach the restaurant, take a short taxi ride from the city center. It's a great spot for a relaxed meal but not typically known for hosting large parties.

For those craving Italian cuisine, **Pizza A La Leña** on Avenida 10, Calle 2 offers some of the best wood-fired pizzas in the area. The thin, crispy crust is topped with fresh, high-quality ingredients. Favorites include the Margherita, made with tomatoes, mozzarella, and basil, priced at $12, and the Quattro Formaggi, featuring a blend of four cheeses for $15. The casual, family-friendly atmosphere makes this pizzeria a perfect spot for a relaxed meal. It's easily reachable by a short walk or taxi ride from downtown. While it's primarily a dining spot, it's lively and welcoming.

Soda El Patio on Avenida 7, Calle 4 is a local gem for quick bites or casual dining. This eatery serves traditional Costa Rican dishes at affordable prices. The arroz con pollo, a simple yet flavorful chicken and rice dish, is a staple costing around $8. Their ceviche, made with fresh fish marinated in lime juice, is another must-try for $7. The laid-back atmosphere and friendly service make it a great place to grab a bite and enjoy the local culture. It's easily accessible on foot or by taxi from the central area.

For dessert, head to **Heladería Luna de Leche** on Avenida 6, Calle 2. This delightful ice cream parlor offers homemade ice creams and sorbets in traditional and unique flavors. Try the guanabana (soursop) or passion fruit sorbet for $3 per scoop, or indulge in the rich chocolate or creamy vanilla. The welcoming atmosphere makes it a perfect spot for a sweet treat after exploring the city. It's conveniently located downtown, making it easy to visit on foot.

Restaurante Finca Rosa Blanca in Santa Bárbara de Heredia offers a unique dining experience set within a stunning coffee plantation. This eco-friendly restaurant focuses on farm-to-table dining, using organic, locally sourced ingredients. The coffee-rubbed steak is a standout dish priced at $25, offering a robust flavor that perfectly complements the tender meat. Enjoy the beautiful surroundings and the restaurant's commitment to sustainability. It's about a 20-minute drive from the city center, best reached by taxi.

Another great choice for local fare is **Café Britt** in Barva, primarily known for its coffee tours. The café serves a variety of Costa Rican dishes, perfect for enjoying alongside their famous coffee. Try the tres leches cake for dessert, a moist and sweet treat made with three types of milk, costing about $5. The café is a 15-minute drive from the center, accessible by taxi. It's a peaceful spot to relax and savor both local food and exceptional coffee.

For a cozy, homestyle dining experience, **Restaurante La Cocina de Lilliana** on Avenida 9, Calle 1 is a must-visit. Known for its traditional Costa Rican soups like olla de carne, a hearty beef and vegetable stew, this restaurant makes you feel right at home. The soup is priced at around $12 and is served in a warm, inviting atmosphere. It's ideal for unwinding after a day of sightseeing. Reach the restaurant easily by a short taxi ride from downtown.

6.Limón

Limón: Caribbean Dreams

To get to Limón from San José, start by taking Route 32, also known as the Braulio Carrillo Highway. This is a scenic drive that takes about three to four hours. Make sure your car is in good condition and has enough gas because there aren't many gas stations along the way. The road goes through beautiful rainforests and mountains, so enjoy the views as you drive.

If you prefer to take a bus, go to the Gran Terminal del Caribe in San José. Buses to Limón leave every hour, starting early in the morning and running until late evening. The bus ride takes about four hours and costs between 3,000 to 4,000 colones (about $5 to $7 USD). Get to the bus station at least 30 minutes before your bus leaves to get a good seat. The bus ride is comfortable and you will see a lot of the countryside.

For a faster option, you can fly from San José to Limón. Domestic flights take about 30 minutes and are offered by airlines like Sansa. Tickets cost between $50 to $100 USD one way. The flight gives you a great view of the coastline and the Caribbean Sea. When you arrive at Limón's small airport, you can take a taxi to the city center.

When you arrive, you will notice the vibrant Afro-Caribbean culture and relaxed atmosphere. Puerto Limón, the main city, is known for its rich history and has been an important port for banana and coffee exports since the late 1800s.

To get around the city, you can use taxis, which are easy to find and not very expensive. Make sure to use the official red taxis with a yellow triangle. The drivers are friendly and can give you tips on where to go. If you want a local experience, take the public buses. They are cheap, usually costing less than 500 colones (about $1 USD), and go to most parts of the city and nearby beaches.

Walking around the city center is also a good option because many attractions, shops, and restaurants are close to each other. Visit the central market to see fresh produce, local crafts, and traditional foods. Be prepared for hot and humid weather by wearing light clothes and drinking plenty of water.

If you want to visit the beaches, like Cahuita or Puerto Viejo, you can take a bus or drive. These beaches are about an hour south of the city. Route 36 will take you there and the drive is pleasant with nice views. Cahuita has a national park with beautiful trails and lots of wildlife. Puerto Viejo is known for its surfing, reggae music, and lively nightlife.

The city has many cultural events. The biggest event is the annual Carnival in October, which has parades, music, and dancing. This is a great time to visit if you want to experience the local culture.

Top Attractions

The Wild Cahuita National Park

To visit Cahuita National Park, start by driving south from San José on Route 32 to Limón, then take Route 36 to the town of Cahuita. The drive takes about four hours in total. If you prefer public transport, catch a bus from the Gran Terminal del Caribe in San José to Limón, then transfer to a bus heading to Cahuita. The bus ride takes around four and a half hours and costs about $7 USD in total.

The main entrance to Cahuita National Park is located in the town of Cahuita. The park is open daily from 6:00 AM to 5:00 PM, and while entrance is free, donations are encouraged to help with conservation efforts.

For snorkeling, head to the coral reef near the park's entrance. This reef is one of the best in Costa Rica, filled with colorful corals and marine life like parrotfish, angelfish, sea turtles, and rays. Guided snorkeling tours, which cost around $20 to $30 USD per person, are highly recommended for safety and to ensure you see the best spots. These tours usually include all necessary gear.

If you love hiking, the Cahuita Point Trail is perfect for you. This trail is about 8 kilometers long and takes you along the coast from the Kelly Creek entrance to Puerto Vargas. The trail is mostly flat and takes about 2 to 3 hours to walk, making it suitable for all fitness levels. As you hike, look out for monkeys, sloths, iguanas, and a variety of birds like toucans and herons. Early morning or late afternoon are the best times to see wildlife, as animals are most active during these cooler parts of the day. Bring plenty of water, a hat, and sunscreen to stay comfortable.

The Kelly Creek Ranger Station at the main entrance provides maps and information. It's a good place to start your visit, especially if you're interested in learning about the best spots to see animals. Walking slowly and quietly will increase your chances of spotting wildlife. Don't forget to bring binoculars and a camera to capture the amazing sights.

Wear comfortable hiking shoes because the trails can be uneven. Also, pack insect repellent to protect yourself from mosquitoes, and consider bringing a light rain jacket, as weather can change quickly. It's a good idea to pack a picnic, as there are many scenic spots along the trail where you can stop to eat and enjoy the view.

While you're in Cahuita, you can also enjoy the town's relaxed Caribbean vibe. There are several small restaurants and shops near the park entrance where you can try local dishes and buy souvenirs.

The Mystical Tortuguero National Park

Tortuguero National Park is a gem of Costa Rica, famous for its stunning canal tours, magical turtle nesting seasons, and excellent visitor facilities. To fully experience the park, you must take a canal tour, which is the best way to see the diverse wildlife in this lush, water-rich environment. Start your adventure in the town of Tortuguero, where numerous small boats with experienced guides are ready to take you through the park's intricate network of canals. These tours usually last about two to three hours and cost around $20 to $30 USD per person. The early morning tours are especially recommended, as this is when the wildlife is most active, and the chances of spotting animals like howler monkeys, three-toed sloths, caimans, and a plethora of bird species are highest.

One of the most enchanting aspects of Tortuguero National Park is its turtle nesting season, a truly unique experience that attracts visitors from around the world. The park is one of the most important nesting sites for green sea turtles, and the nesting season runs from July to October, with the peak in August. During this time, guided night tours allow you to witness the incredible sight of turtles coming ashore to lay their eggs. These tours are carefully managed to protect the turtles, ensuring minimal disturbance. You can expect to pay about $25 USD per person for these guided night tours. Only certified guides are allowed to lead these tours, providing both an educational and respectful experience that benefits the turtles and the environment.

Visitor facilities at Tortuguero National Park are well-maintained and designed to enhance your visit. Near the main entrance, you'll find a visitor center where you can obtain maps, information about the park, and purchase tickets for various tours. This center is an excellent starting point, providing insights and setting the stage for your adventure. Clean restrooms and a small café are available here, offering snacks and drinks to keep you refreshed. If you enjoy hiking, the park features several well-marked trails that allow you to explore the jungle on foot. These trails vary in length and difficulty, providing opportunities for both casual walks and more strenuous hikes, all while surrounded by the vibrant flora and fauna of the region.

Accommodations in the town of Tortuguero cater to all budgets and preferences, from budget-friendly hostels to luxurious eco-lodges. Many of these lodges and hotels offer package deals that include canal tours and turtle watching tours, making it convenient and cost-effective to plan your visit. Given the popularity of the turtle nesting season, it's wise to book your accommodations and tours well in advance to ensure availability.

Reaching Tortuguero requires a bit of planning, as the park is accessible only by boat or plane. From San José, you can take a domestic flight to

Tortuguero, which offers a quick and scenic way to reach the park. Alternatively, many visitors opt for a combination of bus and boat. From San José, you can take a bus to the town of La Pavona, where you can then board a boat that takes you directly to Tortuguero.

Best Accommodations: From Hammocks to Hotels

Hotel Playa Bonita sits right on Playa Bonita beach, offering stunning ocean views and direct access to the sand. Rooms cost between $70 and $120 per night, and you'll enjoy amenities like free Wi-Fi, an outdoor pool, and a restaurant serving local dishes. It's just a 10-minute drive from downtown on Route 32. While you're here, visit Vargas Park to see local plants and flowers, and explore the historic Black Star Line building.

For a unique experience, Almonds and Corals Lodge is nestled between the beach and the rainforest in Manzanillo. This eco-lodge blends into the natural surroundings, with rooms priced from $100 to $200 per night. Enjoy guided nature walks, a spa, and yoga classes. The lodge is about an hour's drive south via Route 36. Nearby, explore the Gandoca-Manzanillo Wildlife Refuge, where you can snorkel and watch birds.

Casa Marbella, located in the heart of Puerto Viejo, offers budget-friendly rooms ranging from $40 to $70 per night. Services include free Wi-Fi, bike rentals, and a communal kitchen. It's a 45-minute drive south along Route 36. In Puerto Viejo, visit Cahuita National Park for hiking and wildlife spotting, and the Jaguar Rescue Center to learn about animal rehabilitation.

Hotel Aguas Claras in Playa Chiquita features beautifully decorated bungalows and suites priced from $150 to $300 per night. Amenities include an outdoor pool, free breakfast, and a private beach area. It's about an hour south, reached by driving on Route 36. Nearby, relax at Punta Uva beach or visit the Sloth Sanctuary.

For a budget option with a unique twist, Rocking J's in Puerto Viejo offers hammocks for $7 per night and private rooms for $30 to $60. This lively hostel includes free Wi-Fi, a communal kitchen, and a bar. It's a 45-minute drive south. Enjoy surfing at Salsa Brava or explore the vibrant nightlife in Puerto Viejo.

Le Cameleon Boutique Hotel in Cocles offers luxury rooms ranging from $200 to $400 per night. The hotel has an outdoor pool, a beach club, and a restaurant with international cuisine. It's about an hour's drive south on Route

36. While here, visit Cocles Beach and the Finca La Isla Botanical Garden.

Cariblue Beach and Jungle Resort in Puerto Viejo combines jungle and beach experiences, with rooms costing between $100 and $200 per night. The resort features an outdoor pool, a spa, and a restaurant. It's about an hour south on Route 36. Visit Cahuita National Park for snorkeling and zip-lining adventures.

Selina Puerto Viejo is another budget-friendly option, with dorm beds starting at $15 and private rooms from $50 per night. The hostel includes a restaurant, a swimming pool, and yoga classes. It's a 45-minute drive south, located near the lively town center where you can explore shops, bars, and restaurants.

Each of these accommodations offers something special, whether you're looking for luxury, charm, or affordability. Enj

Dining Options: Caribbean Flavors

To experience the best Caribbean flavors, start with Restaurant Marisqueria Muellecito near the port area. This spot is known for its fresh seafood. Try the ceviche, with fish marinated in lime juice, onions, and cilantro, served with crispy plantain chips. The grilled fish, often a catch of the day, is tender and full of flavor, paired with coconut rice and mixed vegetables. Shrimp cocktails are another highlight, featuring plump shrimp in a tangy tomato sauce. Prices range from $10 to $20 USD per dish. The friendly staff ensures a pleasant meal. Take a short taxi ride from the city center, and enjoy the view of the bustling port.

Soda El Patty on Avenida 3 is perfect for authentic local dishes. They serve rice and beans cooked in coconut milk, jerk chicken, and patty pastries filled with spiced meat. Meals cost between $5 and $10 USD. The casual and welcoming atmosphere, along with helpful staff, makes it a great spot for a quick meal. It's a short walk from downtown, so it's easy to find.

Café Sierra on Calle 5 offers a relaxing meal with a beautiful view of the sea. The menu includes fresh salads, sandwiches, and seafood. Prices range from $8 to $15 USD. The warm and welcoming staff add to the cozy atmosphere. After a stroll in the central park, it's just a short walk away.

Restaurant Congo's in the Hotel Playa Bonita is an upscale option with a menu blending Caribbean and international flavors. Start with a seafood platter, including shrimp, mussels, and calamari. For the main course, try the lobster with garlic butter or the coconut curry chicken. Prices range from $20 to $40 USD. The knowledgeable staff provides excellent service. The beachfront location offers a spectacular sunset view. It's a 10-minute drive from downtown, easily reached by taxi.

La Uvita, located on the outskirts of the city, specializes in Afro-Caribbean cuisine. Try the rondón, a coconut milk seafood stew served with fried plantains. Prices range from $12 to $25 USD. The staff is friendly, and the atmosphere is lively with local music. Take a taxi to reach this vibrant spot.

For dessert, visit Gelateria Italiana La Dolce Vita on Avenida 2. This ice cream parlor offers homemade gelato in flavors like passion fruit, guava, and chocolate. Each scoop costs about $3. The friendly staff and convenient location near the main shopping area make it a perfect stop to end your meal.

Moving Around Tips

Using taxis is one of the easiest ways to move in the city. Always use official red taxis with a yellow triangle on the side to be sure for your safety. These taxis are metered, and fares are generally reasonable. For short trips within the city, you can expect to pay around $2 to $5 USD. For a trip from the city center to Playa Bonita, the fare is approximately $8 to $10 USD. You can easily hail a taxi on the street or find them at designated taxi stands near major landmarks such as the central market and bus station.

Limón has a reliable and affordable bus system, which is a great way to explore both the city and nearby attractions. The main bus terminal is located at the intersection of Avenida 2 and Calle 4. For traveling within the city, buses are frequent and cost around 300 to 500 colones ($0.50 to $0.80 USD) per ride. For trips to nearby beaches or towns, buses to Cahuita or Puerto Viejo leave from the main terminal. The fare to Cahuita is about 1,500 colones ($2.50 USD), and it takes roughly one hour. The bus to Puerto Viejo costs around 2,000 colones ($3.30 USD) and takes about 1.5 hours.

Walking also is a convenient way to explore downtown, especially for visiting local markets, restaurants, and popular historical sites. The central market, as you may know already, located on Avenida 2, is a hub of activity where you can buy fresh produce, local crafts, and traditional foods. Take a stroll along the waterfront promenade for a scenic view of the Caribbean Sea and to visit Parque Vargas, a lovely park filled with local flora.

Renting a bike is an excellent echo alternative to see more of Limón at your own pace. Look for bike rental shops in the city center, particularly around popular tourist areas. The average cost for renting a bike is about $10 to $15 USD per day. Use the bike to explore the coastal areas or take a leisurely ride through town, enjoying the local sights and sounds.

7.Puntarenas

Getting to Puntarenas

To get to Puntarenas from San José, drive along Route 27. This well-maintained highway takes about one and a half to two hours. Make sure to have some cash for the tolls along the way, which typically cost between 500 and 800 colones each. Fill up your gas tank before you leave San José to avoid any inconveniences.

If you prefer public transportation, head to the Coca-Cola Bus Terminal in San José. Buses to Puntarenas leave frequently, about every hour. The bus ride takes around two hours and costs about $5 USD. These buses are comfortable and offer a relaxing way to travel without the hassle of driving.

For a more scenic route, consider taking the ferry from the Nicoya Peninsula. If you're already in towns like Paquera or Naranjo, the ferry ride offers beautiful views of the Gulf of Nicoya and takes about 70 minutes. The ferry operates multiple times a day, so check the schedule in advance. Arrive early, especially during peak travel times, to ensure you get a spot.

Once you arrive in Puntarenas, moving around in the city is easy. The city is compact and walkable, especially in the downtown and waterfront areas. Stroll along the Paseo de los Turistas, a scenic promenade lined with palm trees, shops, and restaurants. Here, you can enjoy with no doubt the local cuisine, pick up souvenirs, and take in the views of the Pacific Ocean.

For longer distances or if you prefer not to walk, local taxis are readily available. Use official taxis, which are red with a yellow triangle, and agree on a fare or ensure the meter is running before start. Local buses also operate within the city and to nearby attractions. These buses are an economical way to get around, with fares typically costing less than $1 USD.

Attractions

Manuel Antonio National Park

Manuel Antonio National Park is a stunning gem along Costa Rica's Pacific coast, a must-visit destination known for its beautiful beaches, lush hiking trails, and abundant wildlife. To reach this tropical paradise from Puntarenas, drive south along Route 34, a scenic experience that takes about three hours. If you prefer public transport, you can take a bus from Puntarenas to Quepos, the nearest town to the park. From Quepos, it's a short ride by local bus or taxi to the park entrance.

The park welcomes visitors from Tuesday to Sunday, opening its gates at 7:00 AM and closing at 4:00 PM. It remains closed on Mondays. Admission costs $18 USD for foreign adults and $5 USD for children. Given the park's popularity and its daily visitor limit, purchasing tickets in advance is recommended, especially during peak tourist seasons.

Upon entering the park, you'll find a lot of activities to immerse yourself in. The beaches within the park, such as Playa Manuel Antonio and Playa Espadilla Sur, are breathtaking with their pristine white sands and clear blue waters. These beaches are ideal for swimming, sunbathing, and snorkeling. Be sure to bring your own snorkel gear, as the underwater scenes are vibrant with colorful fish and coral formations that provide an enchanting glimpse into marine life.

For those who enjoy hiking, the park offers several well-marked trails suitable for various fitness levels. The main trail, Sendero Principal, is an easy walk connecting the beaches and the park entrance, making it accessible for most visitors. If you seek a more challenging adventure, the Punta Catedral Trail offers not only a workout but also stunning panoramic views of the coastline and the dense forest. As you trek these trails, keep your eyes peeled for the rich wildlife that the park is known for. You might spot playful white-faced capuchin monkeys, the louder howler monkeys, and the leisurely sloths hanging from the trees. Bird enthusiasts will delight in the chance to see toucans, scarlet macaws, and the vividly colored motmots.

Wildlife viewing is one of the major attractions in Manuel Antonio National Park, home to over 100 species of mammals and nearly 200 species of birds. The best times for spotting these creatures are early in the morning or late in the afternoon when they are most active. To enhance your wildlife experience, consider hiring a local guide at the park entrance for around $20 to $30 USD. These guides have an expert eye for spotting animals and can share fascinating insights about the park's flora and fauna, enriching your visit.

Prepare for your visit by packing essentials like plenty of water, snacks, sunscreen, insect repellent, and a hat to protect against the tropical sun. While there are no food vendors inside the park, you will find a variety of restaurants and snack shops just outside the entrance in Quepos, where you can enjoy local cuisine.

The Cloud-Kissed Monteverde Reserve

To get to Monteverde Cloud Forest Reserve from Puntarenas, you start by

driving northeast on Route 1 towards Barranca. After about 17 kilometers, you'll see the exit for Route 606. Take that exit, and then follow the winding mountain road up to Santa Elena. This drive will take you about two to two and a half hours. It's a beautiful journey, with lots of stunning views of the countryside and lush greenery. If you don't feel like driving, there's a bus that goes from Puntarenas to Monteverde. You can catch it at the Puntarenas bus terminal, and it takes about three hours to reach Santa Elena, passing through some really scenic landscapes.

Once you get to Monteverde, you'll want to check out the canopy tours. They're an amazing way to see the forest from above. One of the best options is the Sky Walk. It's a series of suspension bridges and trails, costing around $40 to $60 USD. As you walk along the bridges, you get these incredible bird's-eye views of the canopy. You might see exotic birds, monkeys, and other wildlife up close. If you're looking for more of a thrill, Selvatura Adventure Park has an extensive zip-lining tour. You'll be soaring through the treetops, moving from platform to platform, and getting a unique perspective on the forest's diverse plant and animal life.

Hiking is another must-do activity in Monteverde. The Sendero Bosque Nuboso trail is fantastic. It's about 4.5 kilometers long and takes you through dense cloud forest. The views are stunning, and you'll likely see a variety of wildlife. This trail takes about 2 to 3 hours and is moderately challenging, making it a good choice for most hikers. If you prefer something shorter, the Sendero Pantanoso trail leads to a beautiful swamp area, perfect for bird watching. The Sendero Camino is an easier trail and ideal for families, offering a gentle walk through the forest with plenty of opportunities to spot wildlife.

When you visit, make sure you wear comfortable hiking shoes and bring a rain jacket, as the weather in the cloud forest can change quickly. Also, pack some water and snacks to keep your energy up during the hikes. Mornings are the best time to visit because the wildlife is most active, and the trails are less crowded. I'd recommend hiring a guide for around $20 to $30 USD per person. Guides can give you valuable insights into the ecosystem and help you spot things you might otherwise miss.

The reserve is open daily from 7:00 AM to 4:00 PM. Admission is $25 USD for adults and $12 USD for children. It's a good idea to buy tickets in advance, especially during peak seasons, to make sure you can get in.

Once you're in Santa Elena, you'll find plenty of places to stay, from budget hostels to luxurious eco-lodges. They offer various amenities and are close to the reserve, making it easy to explore. The journey to Monteverde is part of the adventure, with picturesque landscapes and winding mountain roads that add to the experience.

Best Accommodations

Fiesta Resort is an all-inclusive beachfront resort offering a luxurious experience. Imagine waking up to the sound of the waves with prices ranging from $150 to $300 USD per night, depending on the season and room type. The resort features multiple swimming pools, a variety of restaurants serving international and local cuisine, and a relaxing spa where you can unwind. You'll have access to activities like beach volleyball, water aerobics, and nightly entertainment. It's a family-friendly place with a kids' club and playground to keep the little ones entertained. Conveniently located near the ferry terminal, it's perfect for day trips to nearby islands.

Another excellent beachfront option is the DoubleTree Resort by Hilton Central Pacific. Prices here range from $120 to $250 USD per night. This all-inclusive resort provides stunning ocean views, several dining options, and activities such as kayaking, tennis, and evening shows. The resort boasts multiple pools, including one with a swim-up bar, making it a great place to relax and enjoy the sun. Nearby, you can visit the Puntarenas Marine Park or take a leisurely stroll along the Paseo de los Turistas, a lively promenade lined with shops, restaurants, and street vendors.

Hotel Alamar is a fantastic budget-friendly option right by the beach, with prices ranging from $60 to $100 USD per night. It offers comfortable rooms, an outdoor pool, and free breakfast to start your day. Located within walking distance to the central market and several restaurants, it's a great base for exploring the town. Spend your days on the nearby beach or wandering through the local shops and cafes, experiencing the vibrant culture of the area.

Cabinas Madeleine provides a more economical stay, offering simple, clean accommodations starting at $40 USD per night. This guesthouse includes free Wi-Fi, air conditioning, and access to a shared kitchen if you prefer to prepare your own meals. Its central location is just a short walk from the ferry terminal and bus station, making it an excellent base for exploring both the town and surrounding areas.

Hotel La Punta offers a unique stay right at the tip of the Puntarenas peninsula. Prices range from $70 to $130 USD per night, featuring charming rooms with ocean views, a small pool, and a lovely garden area. This hotel is perfect for those seeking a quieter, more intimate experience. The location provides easy access to the beach and the ferry terminal, ideal for island-hopping adventures. Imagine spending your evenings watching the sunset over the water, with the serene sounds of the ocean in the background.

Eco Boutique Hotel Vista Las Islas is located on Isla Caballo, a short ferry ride from Puntarenas, offering a unique eco-friendly experience. Prices range from $100 to $200 USD per night. This hotel features stunning views of the Gulf of Nicoya, an infinity pool, and access to secluded beaches. Activities include kayaking, snorkeling, and nature hikes. Then, you can visit the Puntarenas Marine Park to learn about marine life and enjoy family-friendly activities. The Paseo de los Turistas is perfect for an evening stroll. Day trips to nearby islands like Isla Tortuga are a must, offering opportunities for snorkeling, swimming, and relaxing on pristine beaches. If you like the nature, a trip to the nearby town of Monteverde provides a day of hiking and wildlife spotting in the renowned cloud forest.

Dining Options

The Restaurant El Shrimp Shack is a good choice. It's located right on the Paseo de los Turistas, the main beachfront promenade. Walk along this lively stretch until you see the bright sign and outdoor seating. Known for its fresh seafood, dishes like ceviche and shrimp cocktails are favorites. The garlic shrimp is a must-try, a local favorite, with prices around $10 to $25 per dish. The casual beachfront setting adds to the charm, making it a delightful spot for a meal.

Next, head to Soda La Roca near the central market. From the main bus station, walk towards Avenida 2, and you'll find it on the corner. This spot is famous for traditional Costa Rican dishes. Their casado, which includes rice, beans, plantains, salad, and your choice of meat or fish, is filling and delicious. It costs between $5 and $10 per plate. The seafood rice is packed with fresh ingredients and is a must-try, offering a true taste of local cuisine.

For a more upscale experience, Las Delicias del Puerto on Calle 1 is perfect. To reach it from the central market, head towards the waterfront and turn left onto Calle 1. This elegant restaurant serves a variety of seafood dishes, including lobster, red snapper, and seafood pasta. The seafood platter is great for sharing and highlights the best of the local seafood. Prices range from $20 to $40 per dish. The refined setting and attentive service make it ideal for a special night out.

Marisqueria La Ostra is a laid-back option with a stunning view, located on the eastern end of the Paseo de los Turistas, near the ferry terminal. Walk or take a short taxi ride to this beachfront restaurant specializing in fresh local seafood. The menu includes fried fish and seafood stews, with prices from $12 to $30 per dish. The mixed seafood grill is a standout, offering a selection of the day's freshest catches, and the ocean view adds to the dining experience.

For breakfast or a light lunch, visit Café y Macadamia. It's a bit inland on the road to Monteverde, about a 15-minute taxi ride from the city center. This cozy café serves excellent coffee, fresh pastries, and light meals like sandwiches and salads. The macadamia nut pie is a local favorite and pairs perfectly with a cup of coffee. Prices are reasonable, usually between $5 and $15. The relaxed atmosphere and delicious treats make it a great spot to start your day.

Finish your culinary tour with a visit to Heladeria Monteverde, a charming ice cream shop near the Paseo de los Turistas. From the central bus station, walk towards the beach and continue along the promenade until you find it. They offer homemade ice cream in flavors like mango and passion fruit. Prices are around $2 to $4 per scoop, making it a perfect treat to enjoy as you stroll along the beachfront, taking in the sights and sounds of the lively promenade.

Tips for Moving Around

Puntarenas is relatively small, covering an area of about 60 square kilometers, with a population of approximately 35,000 people. This compact size makes it quite easy to get around.

The main part of Puntarenas is very walkable. Most attractions, restaurants, and shops are within easy walking distance from each other, especially along the main drag, Paseo de los Turistas. You'll find that comfortable shoes are a must, as you'll likely spend a lot of time on your feet exploring the charming streets and vibrant waterfront. This seaside promenade stretches along the beachfront, making it a pleasant area to stroll, dine, and shop.

For longer distances or if you prefer not to walk, taxis are a convenient option. Look for the official red taxis with a yellow triangle on the side. These are reliable and safe. It's best to agree on a fare before starting your journey or ensure the meter is running. A short trip within town typically costs around $2 to $5 USD, depending on the distance. Taxis are easy to hail on the street, or you can find them at taxi stands near major attractions and transportation hubs.

If you're planning to explore nearby areas, the bus system is both reliable and affordable. The main bus terminal is centrally located on Avenida Central. From there, you can catch buses to various destinations, including San José, Monteverde, and other coastal towns. Buses to San José depart frequently, and tickets cost about $5 to $8 USD, with the journey taking around two hours. For Monteverde, buses are less frequent but provide a scenic route through the mountains, offering breathtaking views along the way.

8. Guanacaste

To reach the sun-drenched beaches of Guanacaste, you have a few excellent options. If you prefer to fly, the Daniel Oduber Quirós International Airport in Liberia is the primary gateway. This airport receives direct flights from many major cities, making it a convenient starting point. Once you land, you can rent a car right at the airport or take a taxi to your destination. Renting a car is a great choice if you plan to explore multiple beaches and towns, giving you the freedom to travel at your own pace and visit some of the more secluded spots along the coast.

If you prefer driving from San José, the trip takes about four to five hours, depending on your final destination within the province. The route along the Inter-American Highway (Route 1) is straightforward and scenic, offering picturesque views of Costa Rica's countryside. Having your own vehicle allows you to stop and enjoy the sights along the way, from quaint villages to panoramic vistas, making the drive part of your adventure.

For those who prefer public transportation, buses are a reliable and economical option. Buses from San José to various towns in the province can take between five to seven hours. Departing from the main bus terminal in San José, these buses are generally comfortable and provide an affordable means of travel. It's wise to check the schedule and buy tickets in advance, especially during peak travel times..

Guanacaste, located in the northwestern part of Costa Rica, is a large province known for its stunning coastline along the Pacific Ocean. Liberia, the capital city, has a population of around 60,000 people. This province is less densely populated than other regions, featuring expansive rural areas and numerous small beach towns. The region is steeped in history and culture, with a rich blend of indigenous Chorotega heritage and Spanish colonial influences. Traditional music, dance, and cuisine are integral to the local culture, offering a vibrant backdrop to your travels.

The province is characterized by its dry tropical climate, which sets it apart from the more humid regions of Costa Rica. The dry season, running from November to April, is ideal for visitors who prefer sunny, rain-free days. During this time, the weather is perfect for beach activities and exploring outdoor attractions. Conversely, the wet season, from May to October, brings lush greenery and fewer tourists, providing a different kind of beauty and tranquility.

Local festivals are fantastic. The Fiestas Civicas in Liberia, held in late February or early March, is a week-long celebration featuring rodeos, traditional bullfighting, parades, music, and dancing.

While you're here, make sure to explore the beautiful beaches such as Playa Tamarindo, Playa Conchal, and Playa Hermosa. Each beach offers its own unique charm, from the bustling surf scene in Tamarindo, where you can take surfing lessons or simply watch the waves, to the serene, white sands of Conchal, perfect for a peaceful day of relaxation. Water activities like snorkeling and scuba diving are also popular, with plenty of local shops offering equipment rentals and lessons.

Attractions

The Rugged Rincon de la Vieja National Park

Rincon de la Vieja National Park is an incredible destination filled with adventure and natural beauty. To reach the park from Liberia, you'll need to drive northeast on Route 1 for about 25 kilometers until you reach the turnoff for Route 913, which will take you directly to the park entrance. The drive typically takes around an hour and is well-marked, making it straightforward to navigate.

When you arrive at the park, you can purchase your admission tickets at the entrance. The fee is $15 USD for adults and $5 USD for children. The park is open daily from 7:00 AM to 3:00 PM, and it's a good idea to arrive early to avoid the heat and see more wildlife.

The volcano tours are one of the park's main attractions. These guided tours, costing between $45 to $65 USD per person, will take you through diverse landscapes, including tropical forests and volcanic craters. You'll encounter geothermal features such as fumaroles, boiling mud pots, and steam vents. For those feeling adventurous, some tours include a hike to the crater rim, offering breathtaking views of the surrounding area. Wear sturdy hiking boots, as the terrain can be rugged, and carry plenty of water to stay hydrated.

After exploring the volcano, head to the hot springs in the Las Pailas area. The entrance to these natural hot springs is included in your park admission fee. The hot springs are heated by the volcano and rich in minerals, providing a soothing and relaxing experience. To reach them, you'll take a short, scenic hike through lush forest. If you prefer a more private experience, some tours offer access to secluded hot springs for an additional fee.

For hiking enthusiasts, the park offers several excellent trails. The Las Pailas loop trail is a favorite, spanning about 3.5 kilometers and taking around two hours to complete. This relatively easy hike is suitable for most fitness levels and offers views of geothermal features, waterfalls, and wildlife such as monkeys and toucans. It's a great introduction to the park's diverse ecosystem.

If you're up for a more challenging adventure, the trail to La Cangreja Waterfall is a must. This hike is approximately 10 kilometers round trip and takes around five hours to complete. The trail winds through dense forest, across rivers, and up steep inclines, leading to a stunning 130-foot waterfall with a crystal-clear pool at its base. The hike is strenuous, so be prepared with good hiking shoes, plenty of water, and snacks. The effort is rewarded with the beauty of the waterfall and a refreshing swim in its pool.

Another notable trail is the hike to the Santa Maria sector, which includes a visit to the historical Santa Maria ranger station. This trail is around 7 kilometers long and offers a mix of moderate and challenging sections. Along the way, you'll pass through various ecosystems and see a variety of wildlife. The ranger station itself provides interesting historical context about the park.

When visiting Rincon de la Vieja, it's important to pack the right gear. Essentials include plenty of water, snacks, sunscreen, insect repellent, and a hat to protect yourself from the sun. Wear comfortable hiking clothes and sturdy boots to navigate the trails safely. If you plan to soak in the hot springs, bring a swimsuit and a towel.

For those relying on public transportation, buses run from Liberia to the park. You can catch a bus from the Liberia bus terminal to the town of Curubandé, which is near the park entrance. From there, you may need to take a short taxi ride to reach the park itself. Bus schedules can vary, so it's a good idea to check the times in advance.

The Sun-Drenched Tamarindo Beach

Well, If you love surfing, this beach is perfect. It's big, about three kilometers long, and has great waves for everyone. If you're just starting out, you can take lessons from surf schools like Witch's Rock Surf Camp and

Iguana Surf. They also rent out boards. If you're more experienced, head to Pico Pequeno or El Estero. Pico Pequeno is near the rocks at the north end of the beach, and El Estero is where the river meets the ocean. These spots have bigger waves, especially at high tide, which is the best time to surf. Check the local tide charts before you go.

Besides surfing, there's lots to do on Tamarindo Beach. You can sunbathe on the sandy shore, play beach volleyball, or take a long walk. The water is warm and clear, perfect for swimming and snorkeling. If you want to see more of the coast, rent a kayak or a stand-up paddleboard. You can find rentals at different spots along the beach. For something special, take a boat tour. Companies like Blue Dolphin Sailing and Marlin del Rey offer trips that include snorkeling, fishing, and sunset cruises. You might even see dolphins!

When the sun goes down, Tamarindo's nightlife starts. The town is full of lively bars, restaurants, and clubs. Try a cocktail at Nogui's, a bar right on the beach where you can watch the sunset. If you want to dance and enjoy live music, go to Pacifico Bar or Sharky's Sports Bar. La Oveja Negra is also great for live performances and a fun crowd.

Eating in Tamarindo is a joy with many restaurants offering tasty dishes. Try local food like ceviche at Nogui's or grilled fish at Pangas Beach Club. If you want something different, go to Dragonfly Bar & Grill. They have a mix of flavors that you'll love. After dinner, I recommend you to get some ice cream from a local shop and take a walk on the beach. The sound of the waves and the moonlight make for a perfect evening.

Tamarindo also has fun events during the year. The Tamarindo Art Wave is a three-day festival with local and international artists, performances, and workshops.

Accommodations: Ocean Views and Cozy Rooms

For a luxurious stay with beautiful ocean views, stay at the Four Seasons Resort Costa Rica at Peninsula Papagayo. This fancy resort is on the Papagayo Peninsula. The rooms and suites are stunning, with great views of the Pacific Ocean. The resort has many swimming pools, a relaxing spa, and fancy dining options. Rooms start at about $700 per night. You get access to two lovely beaches. To get there, drive from Liberia's Daniel Oduber Quirós International Airport. It takes about 40 minutes and the roads are easy to follow.

If you want something more affordable, the Hotel Tamarindo Diria Beach Resort is a good choice. It's right on Tamarindo Beach, located on Calle Central, Tamarindo. The rooms are comfortable and have balconies with views of the ocean or gardens. The resort has three swimming pools, including a lagoon pool and an adults-only pool. There are also several dining options. Prices range from $150 to $300 per night. The resort is close to shops, restaurants, and nightlife. From Liberia, drive about an hour and 15 minutes along Route 21 and Route 155.

For budget travelers, Cabinas El Colibri in Playa Samara is a great option. This small hotel is just a short walk from Playa Samara and is on Route 160, Samara. Rooms are simple but clean and cost about $50 per night. There's a small pool and a communal kitchen. The staff is friendly and helpful. It's a relaxed place to stay. To get there from Liberia, drive about two hours along Route 21 and Route 150.

If you like staying in hostels, try Selina Tamarindo. It's near Tamarindo Beach on Calle Langosta, Tamarindo. Dorm beds start at $20 per night, and private rooms start at $60 per night. Selina has a lively community vibe, a shared kitchen, co-working space, and activities like yoga and live music. It's a fun place to meet other travelers. The hostel also offers tours. It's easy to walk there from the main bus stop in Tamarindo.

Another good hostel is Pura Vida MINI Hostel in Tamarindo. It's on Calle Principal, Tamarindo. Dorm beds start at $15 per night, and private rooms start at $40 per night. The hostel has a friendly atmosphere and is clean. It's near the beach and town center. There's a garden, a communal kitchen, and organized tours. It's easy to walk to places from the hostel.

For a eco-friendly stay, try the Harmony Hotel in Nosara. This boutique hotel is near Playa Guiones, Nosara. Rooms start at $250 per night. The hotel focuses on being eco-friendly and offers yoga classes, an organic restaurant, and a spa. The setting is peaceful, with tropical gardens and nature sounds. To get there, drive about two and a half hours from Liberia along Route 21 and Route 160.

Dining Options: Beachside Bites

If you want to enjoy a meal by the beach, head to Pangas Beach Club in Tamarindo. This restaurant sits right on the sand, offering you stunning ocean views and a relaxed atmosphere. Picture yourself surrounded by the gentle sound of waves and the warm glow of the sunset. The menu has a variety of fresh seafood. The grilled fish is outstanding, and the ceviche is bursting with zesty flavors. For a true treat, order the seafood platter—it's perfect for sharing and gives you a taste of the ocean's best offerings.

In Playa Samara, El Lagarto is the go-to spot for grilled meats and seafood. This beachfront restaurant features an open grill right in the center, adding a unique touch to your dining experience. The mixed grill platter includes various meats and seafood, all cooked to perfection. The atmosphere is casual and friendly, making it a great place for a relaxed meal with family or friends.

To taste traditional Costa Rican cuisine, visit Soda La Plaza in Liberia. This small, family-run restaurant serves hearty, homemade dishes that give you an authentic taste of local flavors. The casado is a typical dish featuring rice, beans, plantains, salad, and your choice of meat or fish. Another popular dish is the arroz con pollo, a flavorful chicken and rice meal. Portions are generous, and prices are reasonable, perfect for a casual, authentic meal.

At Coco Loco in Playa Flamingo, you can dine with your toes in the sand. Located right on the beach, this restaurant's seafood is the highlight. Try the coconut shrimp, which is crispy and full of flavor, or the fresh mahi-mahi. Pair your meal with a cocktail like the Coco Loco, served in a fresh coconut for a tropical twist.

La Luna in Nosara is a favorite among locals and tourists alike. Set on Playa Pelada, this charming restaurant offers Mediterranean-inspired dishes with a Costa Rican twist. You can enjoy the sea breeze and the soothing sounds of the ocean as you dine. The seafood pasta, packed with fresh, local seafood, is a standout dish. The setting is perfect for a laid-back yet memorable meal.

For a casual dining experience, visit Taco Star in Playa Grande. This food truck serves some of the best tacos in the area. The fish tacos, made with fresh, local catch, offer a perfect blend of flavors and textures. They also have shrimp and beef tacos, all served with homemade salsas that add a delicious kick. It's a great spot for a quick and tasty meal after a day at the beach.

In Playa Avellanas, Lola's is a must-visit. Named after the resident pig, this beachfront restaurant is known for its laid-back vibe and delicious food. The wood-fired pizzas are a standout, with a perfect crust and fresh toppings. The salads are also excellent, featuring crisp, fresh ingredients. With its beachside location, Lola's is the perfect place to relax, enjoy good food, and take in the beautiful surroundings.

For a special dining experience, visit Villa Deevena in Playa Negra. This fine dining restaurant focuses on fresh, local ingredients. The menu changes regularly to highlight the best of what's available. Dishes like seared tuna, lobster risotto, and decadent desserts are prepared with care.

Moving Around Tips

Renting a car is the best way to explore, giving you the freedom to visit beaches, parks, and towns at your own pace. You can rent a car at the Daniel Oduber Quirós International Airport in Liberia or in major towns like Tamarindo and Nosara. Make sure to book in advance, especially during the high season from December to April.

If you don't want to drive, buses are a reliable and affordable alternative. They connect most towns and cities. The main bus terminal in Liberia offers routes to many destinations, including Tamarindo, Nosara, and Samara. Buses are cheap, but travel times can be long due to frequent stops. Check schedules online or at the terminal.

Taxis and ride-sharing services like Uber are available in larger towns and tourist areas. Taxis are usually red with a yellow triangle on the door. Always confirm the fare before starting your trip or ensure the meter is running. Uber can be a convenient option, but availability may be limited outside major towns.

For short distances or trips within a town, biking and walking are also great alternatives. Many towns, especially coastal ones, have bike rental shops. Tamarindo, for example, is very bike-friendly with many paths and bike lanes.

9. Costa Rica Travel Tips

Best Time to Visit

Costa Rica's climate is tropical, and there are two main seasons to consider when planning your visit: the dry season and the rainy season. The dry season runs from December to April, and this is when you'll find the most sunshine and the least rain. It's perfect for beach activities, like swimming, sunbathing, and water sports. Places like Guanacaste and the Pacific coast are at their best during these months. However, this is also the peak tourist season. Popular spots like Manuel Antonio and Arenal Volcano can get crowded, and prices for hotels and tours are higher. Booking in advance is a good idea to ensure you get the accommodation and activities you want.

The rainy season lasts from May to November. While it does rain almost daily, the showers usually come in the afternoon, leaving the mornings clear. This season turns the landscape lush and green, making it ideal for nature lovers and photographers. Waterfalls are fuller, and the forests are vibrant. If you visit during the rainy season, you'll find fewer tourists, which means less crowded attractions and lower prices for accommodation and tours. This can be a great time to explore the natural beauty of Costa Rica in peace. Just remember to pack waterproof clothing and plan your outdoor activities for the morning.

May and November are transitional months. In May, the rains are just beginning, so you might still enjoy some dry days. November is when the dry season starts to take over, offering a mix of rain and sunshine. These months can be a sweet spot for visitors who want to experience the best of both worlds with fewer tourists and beautiful scenery.

The Caribbean coast, including places like Puerto Viejo and Cahuita, has a more consistent climate with rain spread throughout the year. The driest months on this side are September and October, making it a good time to visit if you want to enjoy the beaches and explore the underwater world with activities like snorkeling and diving.

When planning your trip, think about what you want to do. If you love sunny days and lots of beach time, aim for the dry season. If you prefer lush landscapes, fewer crowds, and don't mind a bit of rain, the rainy season will suit you better. Both seasons are a must!

What to Bring

Pack lightweight clothing like t-shirts, shorts, and dresses to stay cool in the warm weather. Bring a rain jacket or poncho because sudden tropical showers can happen, especially during the rainy season. Swimsuits are a must for the beautiful beaches and hotel pools. Comfortable walking shoes are great for exploring towns and cities, and flip-flops or sandals are perfect for the beach and casual outings. If you plan to hike, make sure to bring sturdy hiking boots to handle the trails in the national parks. Also, pack a light sweater or jacket for cooler evenings, particularly in higher elevations like Monteverde.

Bring a wide-brimmed hat and a good pair of sunglasses to shield your face and eyes from the intense tropical sun. Use sunscreen with a high SPF to prevent sunburn, especially since you'll be spending a lot of time outdoors and Insect repellent to avoid bites from mosquitoes and other bugs, particularly in forested areas and near water. Choose a repellent that contains DEET or another effective ingredient for the best protection.

Getting Around: Planes, Trains, and Automobiles tips

Public buses are a reliable and affordable way to travel between cities and towns. The main bus terminal in San José, Terminal 7-10, has routes to popular destinations like Tamarindo, Manuel Antonio, Monteverde, and Arenal. Buses are comfortable, and fares range from $5 to $15 depending on the distance. For example, a bus trip from San José to Tamarindo costs about $10 and takes around five hours. It's best to check bus schedules online or at the terminal, as they can vary.

If you prefer a quicker option, domestic flights are available. Sansa and Nature Air offer flights between major destinations such as San José, Liberia, Quepos, and Tamarindo. These flights are usually under an hour and cost between $50 and $150 one way.

Renting a car provides the most flexibility. Major rental companies like Alamo, Budget, and Hertz have offices at the international airports in San José and Liberia, as well as in larger towns. Expect to pay around $30 to $60 per day for a basic car. If you're visiting mountainous areas or remote beaches, especially during the rainy season, a four-wheel-drive vehicle is a good choice. Driving from San José to Monteverde takes about four hours, and the last part involves navigating winding, unpaved roads.

Taxis are widely available in cities and tourist areas. Official taxis as I told you before are red with a yellow triangle on the side. Taxi fares are reasonable, with a short trip within a city costing around $2 to $5. In rural areas, taxis might be less available.

Ride-sharing services like Uber operate in San José and some larger towns. Uber can be convenient, offering a set price before your trip starts, but availability may be limited in remote areas. Using Uber in Tamarindo to get to nearby Langosta might be feasible, but in less populated areas, you might need to rely on local taxis.

For short distances or trips within towns, biking and walking especially if you are on budget are excellent options. Many towns, especially coastal ones, have bike rental shops. Renting a bike in Tamarindo, for example, costs around $10 to $20 per day. Walking is also enjoyable in smaller towns and beach areas, where everything is close by.

They also have Boat taxis, and you may have fun traveling along the coast, especially in areas like the Nicoya Peninsula. They connect popular beach towns and offer a unique coastal view. A boat taxi from Jaco to Montezuma, for instance, costs around $40 to $50 and is faster and more scenic than a bus.

Safety Tips

Check if you need any vaccinations. The Centers for Disease Control and Prevention (CDC) recommends vaccines for hepatitis A and B, typhoid, and rabies, especially if visiting rural areas or having extended stays.

Travel insurance covers unexpected medical expenses, trip cancellations, and lost luggage. Look for a policy that includes medical evacuation, as it can be costly if you need to be transported back home due to a serious illness or injury.

In Any way, Costa Rica has good healthcare facilities, especially in major cities like San José and Liberia. Public hospitals provide adequate care, but private clinics and hospitals are preferred by many travelers for their shorter wait times and English-speaking staff. In case of a minor illness or injury, local pharmacies, called "farmacias," can provide medications and advice. Pharmacists are well-trained and can often help with common ailments.

If you need to see a doctor, ask for recommendations from your hotel or local contacts. Many hotels have arrangements with nearby doctors who can visit you if needed. In emergencies, once again, dial 911 for immediate assistance. Ambulance services are available, but in remote areas, response times can be a bit longer.

Mosquito-borne illnesses like dengue fever, Zika, and chikungunya are present in Costa Rica.

Tap water in most parts is safe to drink, but if you have a sensitive stomach, consider drinking bottled water. Always wash your hands before eating and use hand sanitizer when soap and water are not available.

Be cautious with food, especially street food. Make sure it's freshly cooked and served hot. Avoid raw or undercooked meats and seafood. Stick to fruits you can peel yourself to avoid potential contamination.

Crime rates are relatively low, but petty theft and pickpocketing can occur, especially in tourist areas. Keep your valuables secure and be aware of your surroundings. Avoid walking alone at night in unfamiliar areas. Use hotel safes for passports, extra cash, and important documents.

In the ocean, be aware of rip currents, especially on the Pacific coast. Always swim at beaches with lifeguards and heed any warning signs. If you're not a strong swimmer, stick to calmer waters or hotel pools.

Budgeting

Estimating the cost for **Accommodation** For mid-range hotels or eco-lodges,you can spend around $75 per night. These accommodations include amenities like breakfast and Wi-Fi, adding value to your stay. Over 14 nights, this will total approximately $1,050.

Food costs can vary based on where and what you eat. If you have lunch and dinner at mid-range restaurants, budget around $20 per meal. Over 14 days, this will amount to $280. Snacks and drinks can add up, so allocate about $5 per day, which totals $70 for the trip. If your hotel does not include breakfast, budget an additional $10 per day, totaling $140. Therefore, your total food cost for the trip will be approximately $490. Eating at local sodas occasionally can help save money.

Transportation will also be a significant part of your budget. Public buses are the most economical option for long-distance travel. A bus trip from San José to Tamarindo or Manuel Antonio costs around $10. If you take four long-distance bus trips, this will total $40. For short trips within cities, taxis are convenient. Each ride costs about $5. Assuming you take two taxi rides per day for 14 days, the total comes to $140. Renting a car for a few days to explore more remote areas is a good idea. Car rentals cost around $60 per day, including fuel. Renting for five days will amount to $300. Combining these options, your total transportation cost will be around $480.

Activities and Tours, Budget around $50 per day for entrance fees to national parks, guided tours, and excursions like zip-lining or boat tours. Over 14 days, this will total $700.

Miscellaneous Additional expenses can include souvenirs, tips, and other small purchases. Allocate about $100 for these miscellaneous costs. Travel insurance is crucial and costs around $50 for a two-week trip. This will cover you for unexpected medical expenses, trip cancellations, and lost luggage, providing peace of mind during your travels.

Full Trip Cost Estimate Summing up all these expenses, the total estimated cost for a 14-day mid-range trip to Costa Rica will be around $2,870. This includes $1,050 for accommodation, $490 for food, $480 for transportation, $700 for activities and tours, $100 for miscellaneous expenses, and $50 for travel insurance.

10. Adventure Activities

Hiking Trails: Paths to Wonder

Corcovado National Park

Corcovado National Park on the Osa Peninsula is known for its incredible biodiversity. The Sirena Ranger Station trail is about 20 kilometers long, taking you deep into the rainforest where you might see monkeys, tapirs, and possibly even jaguars. Always hike with a guide for safety, as the park is remote and the wildlife can be unpredictable. To reach Corcovado, you can fly into Drake Bay or Puerto Jiménez, then take a boat or a short drive to the park entrance. Guided tours can be booked through local operators in these towns. Entry to the park costs around $15 per day, and guided tours usually start at $80 per person. Staying in lodges in Drake Bay or Puerto Jiménez is convenient, with prices ranging from $50 to $200 per night.

Arenal Volcano National Park

The Arenal 1968 Trail in Arenal Volcano National Park offers a scenic 4-kilometer hike through old lava fields with views of the volcano and Lake Arenal. The terrain is rocky, so wear sturdy shoes. Guided tours can enhance your experience by explaining the volcanic activity and unique ecosystem, and can be booked through hotels in La Fortuna or at the park entrance. The entrance fee is about $15, and guided tours cost around $40. To get to Arenal, fly into San José and take a three-hour drive to La Fortuna. Accommodation in La Fortuna ranges from budget hostels at $20 per night to luxury resorts at $200 per night.

Monteverde Cloud Forest Reserve

Monteverde Cloud Forest Reserve is famous for its biodiversity and misty environment. The Sendero Bosque Nuboso is a 2-kilometer trail through dense forest, with hanging bridges providing canopy views. The trails can be muddy, so waterproof boots are recommended. Guided tours, available at the reserve's visitor center or through local tour companies, help spot rare plants and animals and cost about $25. The entrance fee is around $20. To reach Monteverde, fly into San José and drive about four hours to the reserve. Stay in Santa Elena, where accommodations range from $30 to $150 per night.

Rincón de la Vieja National Park

Rincón de la Vieja National Park features the Las Pailas Trail, a 3-kilometer loop through volcanic landscapes with boiling mud pots and steam vents. Bring plenty of water and sun protection, as it can get hot. Guided tours offer insights into the geothermal features and cost around $50, while the entrance fee is about $15. To get to Rincón de la Vieja, fly into Liberia and drive about 1.5 hours to the park. Accommodations near the park, such as eco-lodges and ranches, range from $50 to $200 per night.

Manuel Antonio National Park

Manuel Antonio National Park's main trail is a 2-kilometer path leading to beaches and viewpoints, perfect for spotting sloths, monkeys, and birds. Visit early to avoid crowds. Guides at the park entrance can enhance your experience, and guided tours cost around $25. The entrance fee is about $16. To reach Manuel Antonio, fly into San José and drive three hours to Quepos. Stay in Quepos or Manuel Antonio, with accommodations ranging from budget hostels at $20 per night to upscale resorts at $250 per night.

Cerro Chirripó

Cerro Chirripó is the highest peak in Costa Rica, offering a challenging 19-kilometer hike starting from San Gerardo de Rivas. This hike is typically done over two days with an overnight stay at Crestones Base Lodge, costing about $40 per night. Be physically fit, bring warm clothing, and pack enough food and water. Hiring a guide is highly recommended and costs around $75. Permits are required and can be obtained through the park's website or local tour operators. To get to Cerro Chirripó, fly into San José and drive four hours to San Gerardo de Rivas. Local lodges cost between $50 and $100 per night.

Cahuita National Park

Cahuita National Park offers an 8-kilometer coastal trail perfect for spotting howler monkeys, raccoons, and various birds. The path is flat and well-marked, making it suitable for families. Guides at the park entrance can provide valuable information and cost around $20. Entry to the park is by donation. To reach Cahuita, fly into San José and take a four-hour drive to the Caribbean coast. Stay in Cahuita town, where accommodations range from $30 to $120 per night.

Surfing Spots

Tamarindo Beach

Tamarindo Beach on the Pacific coast is perfect for surfers of all levels. The waves are consistent, making it a popular spot. To get here, fly into Liberia Airport and take a 1.5-hour drive. Witch's Rock Surf Camp and Tamarindo Surf School offer lessons and board rentals, with rentals costing about $10 to $20 a day. Lessons typically start at $50. Tamarindo has many shops, restaurants, and hotels. Budget hostels start at $20 per night, while luxury resorts can be around $200 per night. Plan to stay for at least three to four days to enjoy surfing and explore the town.

Playa Grande

Playa Grande is just north of Tamarindo and known for its strong waves, better suited for intermediate and advanced surfers. Fly into Liberia Airport and take a 1.5-hour drive or a quick taxi ride from Tamarindo. Frijoles Locos Surf Shop offers lessons and rentals for about $15 per day. Accommodation options include comfortable lodges and small hotels, with prices ranging from $50 to $150 per night. Spend at least two to three days here to fully enjoy the surf and the beautiful, uncrowded beach.

Playa Hermosa

Playa Hermosa near Jaco is famous for its powerful waves, ideal for experienced surfers. Fly into San José Airport and take a 1.5-hour drive to Jaco, then a short taxi ride to Hermosa. Hermosa Surf School offers lessons and rentals at $10 to $20 a day. Stay in nearby Jaco, where budget hotels start at $30 per night and higher-end options are around $150 per night. A stay of three days allows you to enjoy the surf and explore Jaco's vibrant nightlife and dining options.

Santa Teresa

Santa Teresa on the Nicoya Peninsula offers waves for all levels. Fly into Tambor Airport and take a 1.5-hour drive or ferry ride from Puntarenas. Del Soul Surf School and Tropicana Surf School provide lessons and rentals at about $20 per day. Santa Teresa has many cafes, shops, and accommodations, with budget stays starting at $40 per night and luxury options up to $250 per night. Plan for at least four days to enjoy surfing, dining, and the town's lively atmosphere. Renting an ATV or 4x4 is recommended for getting around.

Nosara

Nosara, featuring Playa Guiones, is perfect for beginners and longboarders. Fly into Liberia Airport and drive about 2.5 hours. Nosara Tico Surf School and Safari Surf School offer lessons and rentals for about $15 per day. Nosara is a relaxed town focused on sustainability, with yoga retreats and organic restaurants. Budget accommodations start at $50 per night, while eco-lodges and boutique hotels can go up to $200 per night. Stay for at least four days to enjoy the surf and the town's tranquil atmosphere.

Playa Dominical

Playa Dominical in the south is great for advanced surfers due to its strong waves. Fly into San José Airport and drive four hours to Dominical. Dominical Surf School offers lessons and rentals for $10 to $20 per day. The town has a laid-back feel, with surf shops, bars, and affordable places to stay. Budget accommodations start at $30 per night, while nicer options can be around $100 per night. A three-day stay is ideal to enjoy the surf and the surrounding natural beauty.

Playa Pavones

Playa Pavones, near the Panama border, has one of the longest left-hand waves in the world, perfect for experienced surfers. Fly into San José Airport, then drive about seven hours. Local surf shops offer lessons and rentals for about $15 per day. Pavones is remote and peaceful, with fewer crowds. Budget lodges and small hotels start at $40 per night. Plan to stay for at least three to four days to take full advantage of the long waves and serene setting. The journey is longer, but the unique experience is well worth it.

Wildlife Watching

Corcovado National Park

Corcovado National Park on the Osa Peninsula is a prime spot for wildlife watching. You can see monkeys, tapirs, sloths, and sometimes jaguars. The best time to visit is from December to April when the weather is dry and trails are easier to navigate. To get here, fly into Drake Bay or Puerto Jiménez, then take a boat or a short drive to the park entrance. Entry to the park costs around $15 per day. Guided tours are highly recommended and cost around $80 per person, which includes the guide and sometimes meals. Plan to stay for at least two to three days to fully experience the park. Lodging options in Drake Bay or Puerto Jiménez range from $50 per night for budget accommodations to $200 per night for more luxurious lodges.

Tortuguero National Park

Tortuguero National Park on the Caribbean coast is famous for its sea turtles. The best time to visit is from July to October during the turtle nesting season. You can also see manatees, caimans, and many bird species. To reach Tortuguero, take a boat from La Pavona or fly into the small Tortuguero Airport. Boat tours through the park's canals offer the best chance to see wildlife up close and cost about $50 per person. Entry to the park is $15. Plan to stay for at least two days to explore the canals and watch the turtles. Lodging options in Tortuguero village range from $30 per night for basic hotels to $150 per night for more comfortable lodges.

Monteverde Cloud Forest Reserve

Monteverde Cloud Forest Reserve is perfect for birdwatching, especially for seeing the resplendent quetzal. The best time to visit is from December to April. The drive from San José to Monteverde takes about four hours. Entry to the reserve costs around $20. Guided tours are available for about $25 and can help you spot various bird species, monkeys, and other wildlife. Wear waterproof boots because the trails can be muddy. Plan to stay for at least two to three days to fully explore the reserve. Accommodation options in Monteverde range from $30 per night for budget hotels to $150 per night for more upscale lodges.

Manuel Antonio National Park

Manuel Antonio National Park is known for its easy access to wildlife. You can see sloths, monkeys, iguanas, and many birds. The best time to visit is from December to April when the trails are dry and the animals are more active. Fly into San José and drive about three hours to Quepos. Entry to the park is $16. Guided tours at the park entrance cost about $20 and are great for spotting hidden animals. Plan to stay for at least two days to enjoy the park and its beaches. Accommodations in Quepos and Manuel Antonio range from $20 per night for hostels to $250 per night for luxury resorts.

Cahuita National Park

Cahuita National Park on the Caribbean coast offers a chance to see howler monkeys, raccoons, and various birds. The best time to visit is during the dry months of September and October. Drive four hours from San José to Cahuita. Entry to the park is by donation, typically around $5. Walking along the coastal trail provides excellent opportunities for wildlife spotting. Local guides at the park entrance cost about $15 and can show you the best spots. Plan to stay for at least two days to enjoy the park and nearby beaches. Accommodations in Cahuita range from $30 per night for budget hotels to $120 per night for more comfortable lodges.

La Selva Biological Station

La Selva Biological Station in the Sarapiquí region is a renowned research center. It is a great place to see birds, frogs, and other wildlife. Visit during the dry season from December to April for the best conditions. Drive from San

José, which takes about two hours. Entry to La Selva costs around $30. Guided tours are highly recommended and cost about $40. Plan to stay for at least one to two days to fully explore the station. Lodging options at La Selva range from $50 to $100 per night, depending on the type of accommodation.

Rincón de la Vieja National Park

Rincón de la Vieja National Park is known for its volcanic landscapes and diverse wildlife, including monkeys, coatis, and various bird species. The best time to visit is from December to April. Drive from Liberia to the park, which takes about 1.5 hours. Entry to the park costs around $15. Guided tours are available for about $40 and help you explore the park's geothermal features and spot wildlife along the trails. Plan to stay for at least two days to fully enjoy the park. Accommodations near the park range from $50 per night for eco-lodges to $200 per night for more luxurious stays.

Zip-lining Locations

Monteverde Cloud Forest Reserve

Monteverde Cloud Forest Reserve is one of the top places for zip-lining in Costa Rica. Selvatura Park offers a canopy tour with 13 cables and 15 platforms, including a breathtaking 1-kilometer-long cable that soars high above the lush forest canopy. To get there, fly into San José and drive about four hours to Monteverde. The cost for the zip-lining tour is about $50 per person. You can book your adventure online through the Selvatura Park website or at local tour offices in Monteverde. Plan to stay at least two to three days in Monteverde to explore other attractions like the hanging bridges and butterfly gardens. Accommodations range from budget hostels starting at $30 per night to luxury lodges at around $150 per night.

Arenal Volcano Area

In the Arenal Volcano area, Sky Adventures offers one of the best zip-lining experiences. The Sky Trek tour includes seven cables, some reaching up to 200 meters high and 750 meters long, providing stunning views of the volcano and Lake Arenal. Fly into San José and drive about three hours to La Fortuna. The cost is around $80 per person. You can book your tour on the Sky Adventures website or through hotels in La Fortuna. Plan to stay at least three days to enjoy other activities like the hot springs and hiking trails. Accommodations in La Fortuna range from $40 per night for budget options to $200 per night for high-end resorts.

Manuel Antonio National Park

Manuel Antonio National Park is another fantastic location for zip-lining. El Santuario Canopy Adventure features the longest single zip-line in Central America, stretching over 1.3 kilometers. The tour includes 11 zip-lines, 3 suspension bridges, and 2 rappel lines. Fly into San José and drive about three hours to Quepos. The cost is approximately $75 per person. Bookings can be made online via the El Santuario website or at local tour agencies in Manuel Antonio. Plan to stay for at least two to three days to explore the park and its beautiful beaches. Accommodations range from $50 per night for budget hotels to $250 per night for luxury stays.

Monteverde Extremo Park

Monteverde Extremo Park is known for its high-adrenaline zip-lining tours. This adventure includes 14 cables, with the longest being 1 kilometer, and a superman cable where you can fly face-down for an extra thrill. Fly into San José and drive about four hours to Monteverde. The price is around $60 per person. Reservations can be made on the Monteverde Extremo Park website or at tour offices in Monteverde. Plan to stay for at least two days to enjoy other activities like bungee jumping and horseback riding. Accommodations range from $30 per night for budget hotels to $150 per night for upscale lodges.

Diamante Eco Adventure Park

Diamante Eco Adventure Park in Guanacaste offers an exciting zip-lining experience with ocean views. The tour includes a 4,461-foot dual zip-line, allowing you to race side by side. Fly into Liberia and drive about an hour to the park. The cost is about $75 per person. Book your adventure on the Diamante website or through hotels in the Guanacaste region. Plan to spend a full day at the park to enjoy other activities like their animal sanctuary and botanical garden. Accommodations in nearby Playa Hermosa or Playa del Coco range from $50 per night for budget hotels to $200 per night for beachfront resorts.

Mistico Arenal Hanging Bridges Park

Mistico Arenal Hanging Bridges Park, located near Arenal Volcano, combines zip-lining with hanging bridges. The park offers a zip-lining tour with 7 cables, providing spectacular views of the rainforest canopy and the

volcano. Fly into San José and drive about three hours to La Fortuna. The cost is approximately $70 per person. You can book online via the Mistico Park website or at local hotels and tour agencies in La Fortuna. Plan to stay for at least two to three days to enjoy other activities like the hanging bridges and guided nature walks.

Accommodations in La Fortuna range from $40 per night for budget options to $200 per night for high-end resorts.

Sky Adventures Monteverde Park

Sky Adventures Monteverde Park is another excellent choice for zip-lining in the cloud forest. The Sky Trek tour features ten cables, including a thrilling superman cable. Fly into San José and drive about four hours to Monteverde. The cost is around $80 per person. Bookings can be made on the Sky Adventures website or at Monteverde hotels and tour offices. Plan to stay at least two days to enjoy other attractions like the Sky Walk and Sky Tram. Accommodations range from $30 per night for budget hotels to $150 per night for upscale lodges.

11. Cultural Experiences

Festivals and Events: Celebrations Galore

Día de los Muertos (Day of the Dead)

Día de los Muertos is on November 2nd. Families honor their loved ones who have passed away by visiting cemeteries to clean graves and place flowers. At home, they create altars with photos, candles, and favorite foods of the deceased. This tradition helps families remember and celebrate the lives of those who have died. To experience this, visit local cemeteries or homes. Most activities are free. Staying in San José or other cities costs about $30 to $150 per night depending on the type of accommodation.

Fiestas de los Diablitos

Fiestas de los Diablitos happens in Boruca and Rey Curre from late December to early January. It celebrates the Boruca people's resistance against the Spanish. People wear devil masks and costumes and reenact battles with traditional music and dancing. To get there, fly into San José and drive about five hours to Boruca. The event is free, but plan to stay in nearby lodges or hotels, which cost about $50 to $100 per night.

Puntarenas Carnival

Puntarenas Carnival takes place in February. It's one of the biggest parties in Costa Rica with parades, live music, dancing, and street performances. People from all over the country come to Puntarenas to join the fun. Fly into San José and take a two-hour drive to Puntarenas. Most carnival activities are free, but budget for food and drinks. Accommodations in Puntarenas range from $40 to $150 per night.

Semana Santa (Holy Week)

Semana Santa, or Holy Week, is the week before Easter. It is a very important religious time with processions and reenactments of the Passion of Christ. Major processions happen in cities like San José, Cartago, and Heredia. Fly into San José to participate in the events. The processions are free to watch. Accommodations in these cities range from $30 to $200 per night, depending on the hotel.

Festival Internacional de las Artes

The Festival Internacional de las Artes (FIA) occurs every two years in March in San José. It's a large arts festival with performances in theater, music, dance, and visual arts. Streets and parks are filled with art and live shows. Fly into San José to join the festival. Many performances are free, but some events may charge a small fee, usually around $10 to $20. Stay in San José where hotels cost between $40 and $200 per night.

Independence Day

Independence Day is celebrated on September 15th. It marks Costa Rica's independence from Spain in 1821. The day starts with the Torch of Freedom being carried across the country, and there are parades with students in traditional costumes, marching bands, and dances. Celebrations are nationwide but are especially big in San José. Fly into San José to take part. The parades are free. Hotels in San José cost between $30 and $150 per night.

Envision Festival

The Envision Festival is held in late February in Uvita. It's a four-day event with music, art, and yoga, held on the beach and focused on environmental sustainability. Fly into San José and drive about four hours to Uvita. Tickets for the festival range from $300 to $600, depending on when you purchase them. Plan to stay in Uvita for the duration of the festival. Accommodation options include camping, which can be booked through the festival, or nearby hotels costing $50 to $150 per night.

Limon Carnival

Limon Carnival happens in October in the city of Limon. It celebrates Afro-Caribbean culture with parades, live music, dancing, and traditional food. To get there, fly into San José and take a three-hour drive to Limon. Most carnival activities are free, but budget for food and local crafts. Hotels in Limon range from $30 to $100 per night.

Día de la Virgen de Los Ángeles

Día de la Virgen de Los Ángeles is celebrated on August 2nd. It's a major religious pilgrimage to the Basilica in Cartago. Thousands of people walk from all over Costa Rica to honor the Virgin of Los Ángeles. The pilgrimage is known as the romería. Fly into San José and drive about 30 minutes to Cartago. Participating in the pilgrimage is free. Accommodations in Cartago range from $40 to $150 per night.

Fiestas Palmares

Fiestas Palmares is a two-week festival in January in Palmares. It features bullfights, horse parades, concerts, carnival rides, and food stalls. Fly into San José and drive about an hour to Palmares. Many events are free, but tickets for concerts and rides cost extra, usually between $10 and $30. Plan to stay in nearby hotels, with prices ranging from $40 to $120 per night.

Art and Craft Markets: Treasures to Find

San José Central Market

San José Central Market is a bustling place in the heart of the capital where you can find a wide range of local crafts, souvenirs, and art. The market has been open since 1880 and offers handmade jewelry, traditional wooden carvings, vibrant textiles, leather goods, local coffee, and spices. Open daily from 6:30 AM to 6:00 PM, it's an ideal spot to experience the lively local culture. To get there, you can take a taxi or public bus within San José. When bargaining, start by offering about 70% of the asking price and negotiate from there. Sellers usually enjoy some friendly haggling, especially if you're buying multiple items. Stay in San José to explore the market, with hotel prices ranging from $30 to $150 per night.

Guaitil Pottery Village

Guaitil is a small village in Guanacaste known for its traditional Chorotega pottery. Artisans use ancient techniques to create beautiful ceramic pieces like vases, plates, and intricate decorative items. Visiting Guaitil lets you see the pottery-making process firsthand and purchase unique pieces directly from the artisans. Fly into Liberia and drive about two hours to reach Guaitil. Prices for pottery vary but are generally reasonable. It's customary to negotiate a bit, but remember these are handcrafted items. Plan to stay nearby in lodges or hotels, which cost about $50 to $100 per night.

Sarchí Artisan Village

Sarchí, located in the Alajuela province, is famous for its brightly painted oxcarts and furniture, iconic symbols of Costa Rican heritage. The village is full of workshops where you can see artisans at work, painting intricate designs on the famous "carretas." You can find everything from small souvenirs to large furniture pieces. Sarchí is about an hour's drive from San José. Prices vary, with small items starting at $10 and larger pieces costing more. Politely haggle for a good deal. Stay in Sarchí or nearby towns with hotel prices ranging from $40 to $100 per night. While in Sarchí, also visit the central park to see the world's largest oxcart.

Feria Verde de Aranjuez

Feria Verde de Aranjuez, held every Saturday morning in San José, is a lively market with organic produce, healthy food, handmade crafts, and eco-friendly products. It's a great place to find unique jewelry, clothing, and home decor items. The market runs from 7:00 AM to 12:30 PM, providing a lively and vibrant atmosphere. Prices are generally fair, but you can often negotiate a small discount, especially if buying multiple items. To get there, you can take a taxi or walk if you're staying nearby. Stay in San José where hotels range from $30 to $150 per night.

Monteverde Art House

Monteverde Art House is a small, charming market in the cloud forest town of Monteverde. It features local artists who sell paintings, handmade jewelry, textiles, and wood carvings. The market is open daily from 9:00 AM to 5:00 PM. Prices might be higher, but the items are unique and high-quality. Bargaining is less common here, but you can try for a small discount. To get to Monteverde, fly into San José and drive about four hours. Plan to stay in Monteverde for a few days to explore other attractions like the cloud forest reserves. Hotel prices range from $40 to $150 per night.

Santa Elena Market

Santa Elena Market, also in Monteverde, is great for local crafts and souvenirs. Open daily, it offers handmade items like textiles, jewelry, and wood carvings. You can also find locally made chocolates and coffee. Sellers are friendly and open to bargaining. Start with an offer around 70-80% of the asking price. To get to Monteverde, fly into San José and drive about four hours. Stay in Monteverde for a few days, with hotel prices ranging from $40 to $150 per night.

Puerto Viejo Artisan Market

Puerto Viejo, on the Caribbean coast, has a vibrant market reflecting Afro-Caribbean culture. Here, you can find colorful clothing, handmade jewelry, and unique decorative items. The market is open daily, with weekends being the busiest. To get to Puerto Viejo, fly into San José and take a four-hour drive. Bargaining is common, so feel free to negotiate prices. Stay in Puerto Viejo with accommodations ranging from $30 to $120 per night. While here, enjoy the local cuisine and beautiful beaches.

La Fortuna Market

La Fortuna Market, near Arenal Volcano, is a delightful place for local crafts. The market features leather products, jewelry, and wooden carvings. It's open daily, especially lively on weekends. Sellers are open to bargaining. Start with a lower offer and negotiate to a fair price. To get to La Fortuna, fly into San José and drive about three hours. Stay in La Fortuna where hotels range from

$40 to $200 per night. While in La Fortuna, visit the hot springs and take a tour of Arenal Volcano.

Nicoya Market

Nicoya Market in Guanacaste is a great spot for local crafts. The market is open daily and offers pottery, textiles, and handmade jewelry. It's less touristy, giving you an authentic experience. Prices are lower, but bargaining is still expected. Fly into Liberia and drive about an hour to Nicoya. Stay in Nicoya or nearby towns with hotel prices from $40 to $120 per night. While in Nicoya, explore the historic colonial church and enjoy local dishes like gallo pinto.

Local Cuisine

Gallo Pinto

Gallo Pinto is a must-try breakfast in Costa Rica. This savory dish combines rice and beans with onions, red peppers, and cilantro, all flavored with Salsa Lizano. It's often served with eggs, sour cream, and tortillas. For a great Gallo Pinto experience, visit Soda Tapia in San José. Located near La Sabana Metropolitan Park, you can easily get there by taxi or bus. Prices are around $5 to $7 per plate. Enjoy the lively atmosphere and quick service – it's a perfect spot to start your day with a hearty meal.

Casado

Casado is a typical Costa Rican lunch. It includes rice, beans, meat (chicken, beef, pork, or fish), and sides like salad, plantains, and sometimes cheese or an egg. For an authentic Casado, try La Posada de las Brujas in Heredia. Located near the National University, this cozy restaurant offers generous portions and rich flavors. A Casado meal costs about $6 to $10. You can reach Heredia by taxi or local bus from San José. Spend some time exploring the charming town after your meal.

Ceviche

Ceviche is made with fresh fish marinated in lime juice, onions, cilantro, and bell peppers. It's served cold and is very refreshing, especially by the coast. For the best ceviche, visit Los Almendros in Puntarenas. This seaside restaurant offers stunning ocean views and fresh seafood. Prices range from $8 to $12. To get to Puntarenas, take a bus or drive about two hours from San José. Spend the afternoon enjoying the beach and the local seafood.

Olla de Carne

Olla de Carne is a beef stew packed with vegetables like potatoes, carrots, plantains, yucca, and corn. It's perfect for cooler climates like Monteverde. Visit Restaurante Tiquicia in Monteverde for a hearty bowl, costing around $8 to $12. Monteverde is about a four-hour drive from San José. Enjoy the scenic drive through the mountains and plan to stay a few days to explore the cloud forests. Local buses or car rentals are good options for getting there.

Arroz con Pollo

Arroz con Pollo is chicken with rice, cooked with vegetables and seasoned with achiote, giving it a distinctive orange color. It's often garnished with peas and red bell peppers. For a delicious Arroz con Pollo, go to Restaurante La Casona del Cafetal in Cartago. This restaurant, located near the Angostura Lagoon, offers beautiful garden views. Prices range from $7 to $10. Cartago is a 30-minute drive from San José, easily reachable by car or bus. Explore the nearby botanical gardens after your meal.

Chifrijo

Chifrijo is a popular bar snack with layers of rice, beans, fried pork (chicharrones), pico de gallo, and avocado. It's flavorful and filling. Try it at Cebolla Verde in San José. This lively spot is located in the Escalante neighborhood, known for its vibrant nightlife. A plate of Chifrijo costs about $6 to $8. You can get there by taxi or bus within San José. Enjoy the local bar scene with friends and sample other traditional snacks.

Tamales

Tamales are made from corn dough filled with pork or chicken, wrapped in banana leaves, and steamed. They are especially popular during Christmas but can be enjoyed year-round. For a good tamale, visit Mercado Central in San José. Various vendors offer their best recipes. Tamales cost around $3 to $5 each. The market is located in downtown San José, easily accessible by public transport or taxi. Spend some time exploring the bustling market and try other local delicacies.

Patacones

Patacones are twice-fried plantain slices, crispy on the outside and soft on the inside. They are often served with black bean dip or pico de gallo. Try them at Soda Viquez in La Fortuna, a charming eatery near Arenal Volcano. A plate of Patacones costs about $3 to $5. La Fortuna is a three-hour drive from San José. Plan to stay a few days to visit the hot springs and take a tour of Arenal

Volcano. Local buses and car rentals are convenient options for getting there.

Rondon

Rondon is a Caribbean stew made with fish, coconut milk, vegetables, and spices. Try it at Miss Edith's in Puerto Viejo. This restaurant, located near the beach, offers a cozy, authentic atmosphere. Prices range from $10 to $15. To get to Puerto Viejo, fly into San José and take a four-hour drive. The town is famous for its laid-back vibe and beautiful beaches, making it a perfect place to unwind. Enjoy the local music and relaxed atmosphere.

Tres Leches Cake

Tres Leches Cake is a popular dessert made with three types of milk: evaporated, condensed, and heavy cream. It's moist, sweet, and often topped with whipped cream. Enjoy a slice at Pastelería Giacomin in San José. This bakery, located near Avenida Central, is a local favorite. Prices for a slice are about $3 to $5. It's easy to visit by taxi or bus. Pair your dessert with a cup of Costa Rican coffee for a perfect afternoon treat.

Chorreada

Chorreada is a sweet corn pancake, usually eaten for breakfast or as a snack. It's made from fresh corn and served with sour cream or cheese. Try it at Mercado Borbón in San José, a vibrant market with many local food stalls. Prices are around $2 to $4 each. The market is in downtown San José, accessible by public transport or taxi. Enjoy the lively market atmosphere and sample other traditional foods.

Empanadas

Empanadas are pastries filled with cheese, beans, or meat. Visit Soda Yogui's in Heredia for delicious empanadas. This popular spot is located near the central park. Prices are around $2 to $3 each. Heredia is just a short drive from San José, easily reachable by taxi or bus. Enjoy walking around the charming town and visiting the local shops.

Cooking Techniques

Costa Rican cooking is simple, using grilling, boiling, and frying. Fresh ingredients are key, with a heavy reliance on local produce and seafood. Spices are used moderately, with Salsa Lizano being a staple for flavor. This tangy sauce is used in many dishes to enhance the taste without overpowering the natural flavors of the ingredients.

Top Restaurants

Soda Tapia (San José): Located near La Sabana Metropolitan Park, this popular diner serves traditional Costa Rican dishes like Gallo Pinto. Prices range from $5 to $10. It's top-rated for breakfast and offers a lively atmosphere. To get there, take a taxi or bus. Try the Gallo Pinto with eggs and sour cream.

La Posada de las Brujas (Heredia): Found near the National University, this cozy restaurant is known for its generous Casado plates. Prices are about $6 to $12. It's a top choice for lunch. Reach it by taxi or local bus from San José. Order the Casado with chicken for a delicious meal.

Los Almendros (Puntarenas): This seaside restaurant offers stunning ocean views and fresh seafood. Located along the main beach road, it's accessible by bus or car from San José. Prices range from $8 to $15. It's highly rated for ceviche. Enjoy the ceviche with a cold drink while watching the waves.

Restaurante Tiquicia (Monteverde): Situated in the cool mountains of Monteverde, this restaurant is perfect for enjoying Olla de Carne. A four-hour drive from San José, it's worth the scenic journey. Prices are around $8 to $12. It's top-rated for hearty meals. Try the Olla de Carne and enjoy the mountain views.

Restaurante La Casona del Cafetal (Cartago): Near the Angostura Lagoon, this restaurant offers beautiful garden views and tasty Arroz con Pollo. It's a 30-minute drive from San José. Prices range from $7 to $12. It's a favorite for lunch. Order the Arroz con Pollo and stroll through the gardens.

Cebolla Verde (San José): Located in the vibrant Escalante neighborhood, this spot is known for its flavorful Chifrijo. Prices are about $6 to $10. It's popular for evening snacks and drinks. Reach it by taxi or bus. Enjoy the Chifrijo with a local beer.

Mercado Central (San José): This central market is ideal for trying tamales and other traditional foods. Prices are around $3 to $7 per item. It's top-rated for an authentic market experience. Easily accessible by public transport or taxi. Try a tamale from one of the many vendors.

Soda Viquez (La Fortuna): Near Arenal Volcano, this charming eatery is known for its Patacones. Prices range from $3 to $7. It's a top choice for casual dining. A three-hour drive from San José, plan to stay a few days. Order Patacones with black bean dip.

Miss Edith's (Puerto Viejo): This restaurant, located near the beach, is best for Caribbean dishes like Rondon. Prices are $10 to $15. It's a favorite for authentic flavors. A four-hour drive from San José, stay and enjoy the relaxed vibe. Try the Rondon and enjoy the local music.

Pastelería Giacomin (San José): Located near Avenida Central, this bakery is famous for its Tres Leches Cake. Prices are $3 to $6 per slice. It's top-rated for desserts. Easily visit by taxi or bus. Enjoy a slice of Tres Leches Cake with a coffee.

Mercado Borbón (San José): This market is great for Chorreada and other local snacks. Prices are $2 to $5 each. It's a favorite for traditional foods. Located in downtown San José, easy to reach. Try a Chorreada with sour cream.

Soda Yogui's (Heredia): Near the central park, this spot is known for its delicious empanadas. Prices are $2 to $4 each. It's popular for quick snacks. A short drive from San José, easy by taxi or bus. Order an empanada with cheese or beans.

Cooking Classes: Learn to Cook Like a Tico

Costa Rica Cooking School (Tamarindo)

Costa Rica Cooking School in Tamarindo is a fun place to learn how to cook local dishes. Located near the beautiful beaches, it's easy to get there by car or local bus from nearby towns. The school is just a short walk from the main beach area, making it convenient if you're staying in Tamarindo. Classes cost around $75 per person and include all the ingredients and recipes. You'll learn to make Gallo Pinto, Casado, ceviche, and Tres Leches Cake. The chef will guide you step-by-step, and after cooking, you'll enjoy the meal you made. Wear comfortable clothes and be ready to spend a few hours cooking and tasting delicious food. It's a great way to spend a day in Tamarindo, especially if you love the beach and want to experience local culture.

Rainforest Cooking Classes (La Fortuna)

Rainforest Cooking Classes in La Fortuna offers a unique cooking experience in the lush rainforest. Classes cost about $85 per person. You start with a tour of a local farm to pick fresh ingredients. The farm is about a 15-minute drive from the main town, and transportation is often included in the class fee. Then, you learn to cook dishes like Arroz con Pollo, Patacones, and fresh fruit desserts. The classes are small, so you get lots of attention from the chef. To get to La Fortuna, drive or take a bus for three hours from San José. The town itself is full of activities like hot springs, waterfalls, and hiking trails around Arenal Volcano, making it a perfect spot to stay for a few days. Remember to bring a hat and sunscreen for the farm tour.

Tropical Cooking School (Manuel Antonio)

Tropical Cooking School in Manuel Antonio is known for its cooking classes near the national park. You can get there by taxi or local bus. The school is located in the heart of Manuel Antonio, close to many hotels and the main beach. Classes cost about $90 per person and last several hours. You'll learn to make dishes like Olla de Carne, Chifrijo, and Caribbean-style fish. The classes are small, ensuring personalized attention. After cooking, you'll sit down with your classmates and enjoy the meal you've prepared. Manuel Antonio is also known for its beautiful beaches and abundant wildlife, so plan to explore the park and relax on the beach. Wear comfortable shoes and light clothing for the cooking class.

Culinary Tamarindo (Tamarindo)

Culinary Tamarindo offers cooking classes using local ingredients. The school is centrally located in Tamarindo, making it easy to walk to if you're staying nearby or to reach by local transport. Classes cost about $70 per person. You'll learn to cook traditional recipes like Casado, ceviche, and tropical desserts. The atmosphere is relaxed and friendly, and you get to enjoy a meal with your classmates at the end of the class. Tamarindo is a vibrant beach town with plenty of activities like surfing, snorkeling, and shopping. Plan to spend a few days here to fully enjoy the beach life. Bring a camera to capture your cooking experience and the beautiful surroundings.

Sabor Aventura (Monteverde)

Sabor Aventura in Monteverde combines cooking with adventure. Located in the cloud forest, classes cost around $80 per person. You start with a farm tour to gather fresh ingredients, then cook dishes like Gallo Pinto, tamales, and vegetable soups in an open-air kitchen with stunning forest views. Monteverde is about a four-hour drive from San José. The road can be bumpy, so a 4x4 vehicle is recommended. The town is known for its cloud forests, hanging bridges, and zip-lining adventures, so plan to stay a few days. Bring a jacket, as it can get chilly in the evenings, and wear sturdy shoes for the farm tour and cooking class.

Cooking with Grandma (San José)

Cooking with Grandma in San José offers a cozy and unique experience. Classes cost about $65 per person and take place in a local grandmother's home. You'll learn to cook traditional dishes like empanadas, Gallo Pinto, and rice pudding. The classes are small, ensuring a personalized experience. The location is easy to reach by taxi or public transport within San José. The city itself has many cultural attractions, like museums and parks, so spend some time exploring. Bring a notepad to jot down the recipes and tips from Grandma, and don't forget to ask questions about Costa Rican cooking traditions.

The Cooking Spot (Puerto Viejo)

The Cooking Spot in Puerto Viejo is perfect for learning Caribbean cuisine. Classes cost about $75 per person. You'll learn to make dishes like Rondon, coconut rice, and plantain-based desserts. The school is near the beach, making it a great addition to a coastal vacation. After cooking, enjoy your meal with an ocean view. To get to Puerto Viejo, fly into San José and drive about four hours. The town is known for its relaxed vibe and beautiful beaches, so plan to stay a few days. Bring swimwear to enjoy the beach after your cooking class and don't forget your sunscreen.

Green House Cooking School (Arenal)

Green House Cooking School in Arenal offers eco-friendly cooking classes. Prices are around $80 per person. The experience starts with a farm tour to pick organic ingredients. You'll learn to cook dishes like Arroz con Pollo, yucca fries, and tropical fruit salads. The school is set in a beautiful location with views of Arenal Volcano. Classes are small and personalized, ensuring you get plenty of attention from the instructor. La Fortuna, the nearest town, is a three-hour drive from San José. Stay a few days to visit the hot springs and explore the volcano area. Bring a reusable water bottle and comfortable clothes for the farm tour and cooking session.

Bonus Short Chapter

Handy Spanish Phrases

Spanish is a popular language spoken by many people around the world. It shares similarities with Italian, Portuguese, and French since they all come from Latin. It's phonetic, so words are pronounced as they are spelled, making reading and speaking simple. The grammar rules are straightforward with fewer exceptions than English. Nouns have genders, being either masculine or feminine. Many English words resemble Spanish ones, which aids in learning.

Greetings

- **Hello**: "Hola" (oh-lah)
- **Good morning**: "Buenos días" (bweh-nohs dee-ahs)
- **Good afternoon**: "Buenas tardes" (bweh-nahs tahr-dehs)
- **Good evening/night**: "Buenas noches" (bweh-nahs noh-chehs)
- **Goodbye**: "Adiós" (ah-dee-ohs)
- **Please**: "Por favor" (pohr fah-vohr)
- **Thank you**: "Gracias" (grah-see-ahs)
- **You're welcome**: "De nada" (deh nah-dah)

Directions

- **Where is…?**: "¿Dónde está…?" (dohn-deh ehs-tah)
- **How do I get to…?**: "¿Cómo llego a…?" (koh-moh yeh-goh ah)

- **Left**: "Izquierda" (ees-kee-ehr-dah)
- **Right**: "Derecha" (deh-reh-chah)
- **Straight ahead**: "Todo recto" (toh-doh rehk-toh)
- **Near**: "Cerca" (sehr-kah)
- **Far**: "Lejos" (leh-hohs)

Dining

- **A table for two, please**: "Una mesa para dos, por favor" (oo-nah meh-sah pah-rah dohs pohr fah-vohr)
- **The menu, please**: "El menú, por favor" (ehl meh-noo pohr fah-vohr)
- **I would like…**: "Quisiera…" (kee-see-eh-rah)
- **Water**: "Agua" (ah-gwah)
- **Beer**: "Cerveza" (sehr-veh-sah)
- **Check, please**: "La cuenta, por favor" (lah kwehn-tah pohr fah-vohr)
- **Delicious**: "Delicioso" (deh-lee-see-oh-soh)

Emergency Situations

- **Help!**: "¡Ayuda!" (ah-yoo-dah)
- **I need a doctor**: "Necesito un doctor" (neh-seh-see-toh oon dohk-tohr)
- **Call the police**: "Llame a la policía" (yah-meh ah lah poh-lee-see-ah)
- **I'm lost**: "Estoy perdido/perdida" (ehs-toy pehr-dee-doh/pehr-dee-dah) [use "perdido" if you're male and "perdida" if you're female]
- **I don't feel well**: "No me siento bien" (noh meh see-ehn-toh byen)
- **My phone was stolen**: "Me robaron el teléfono" (meh roh-bah-rohn ehl teh-leh-foh-noh)
- **I need help**: "Necesito ayuda" (neh-seh-see-toh ah-yoo-dah)

Common Phrases

- **How much does it cost?**: "¿Cuánto cuesta?" (kwahn-toh kwes-tah)
- **What time is it?**: "¿Qué hora es?" (keh oh-rah ehs)
- **I don't understand**: "No entiendo" (noh ehn-tyen-doh)
- **Do you speak English?**: "¿Habla inglés?" (ah-blah een-glehs)
- **Yes**: "Sí" (see)
- **No**: "No" (noh)
- **Excuse me**: "Disculpe" (dees-kool-peh)
- **Can you help me?**: "¿Puede ayudarme?" (pweh-deh ah-yoo-dar-meh)

Events and Festivals

- **Festival de la Luz**: Held in December in San José, this festival features a grand parade with lights, floats, and music. Ask "¿Dónde está el Festival de la Luz?" (dohn-deh ehs-tah ehl fehs-tee-vahl deh lah loos) to find the location.
- **Día de los Boyeros**: Celebrated in March in Escazú, this festival honors ox cart drivers with parades and traditional foods. "¿Cómo llego a Escazú para el Día de los Boyeros?" (koh-moh yeh-goh ah ehs-kah-soo pah-rah ehl dee-ah deh lohs boh-yeh-rohs) will help you get there.
- **Limon Carnival**: A vibrant celebration in October featuring Afro-Caribbean culture, music, and dance. "¿Dónde está el Carnaval de Limón?" (dohn-deh ehs-tah ehl kahr-nah-vahl deh lee-mohn) will direct you to the festivities.
- **Fiestas de Palmares**: A January festival with bullfights, concerts, and rodeos in Palmares. "¿Cómo llego a Palmares para las fiestas?" (koh-moh yeh-goh ah pahl-mah-rehs pah-rah lahs fyehs-tahs) is useful for finding your way.
- **Envision Festival**: An eco-friendly festival in February in Uvita, combining music, yoga, and workshops. "¿Dónde está el Festival Envision?" (dohn-deh ehs-tah ehl fehs-tee-vahl ehn-vee-syohn) will help you locate it.

Conclusion

Thank you so much for using this guide to help plan your trip to Costa Rica. I put a lot of effort into creating it, researching, and writing to make sure you have the best information. Now that you've read it, you can start planning your trip in detail.

First, decide which cities and attractions you want to visit. Think about what activities you enjoy the most, like relaxing on the beach, exploring rainforests, or visiting cultural sites. Make a list of these places so you can organize your trip better.

If you need more information, look up maps of the areas you want to visit. Maps can help you understand how to get from one place to another. Also, read recent reviews of hotels, restaurants, and tours to get the latest tips from other travelers. Check for any travel updates or advisories before you go.

Here are some fun facts about Costa Rica and its language:

- Costa Rica means "Rich Coast" in Spanish. Early explorers thought the land was rich in gold.
- Costa Rica has no army. The country decided to invest in education and healthcare instead.
- The phrase "Pura Vida" means "pure life." It's a way of life in Costa Rica that emphasizes being happy and relaxed.
- Spanish is the main language, but many people also speak English, especially in tourist areas.
- Costa Rica has more than 5% of the world's biodiversity. It's a small country but very rich in plant and animal life.

I am planning to visit Costa Rica again in [insert month/year]. I'm excited to explore more of this beautiful country and enjoy its culture and nature. I hope this guide helps you have an amazing trip full of wonderful experiences.

p.s if you liked and want to encourage my work, leave a feedback if you bought this guide online.

Thank You,
Sara Palma

ABOUT THE AUTHOR

Thanks for joining me on this incredible journey through Costa Rica! I'm the local expert and enthusiastic guide behind the words that have accompanied you across vibrant landscapes and into the heart of "Pura Vida." Living and breathing this beautiful country has not only been my everyday reality but also my greatest passion.

After years of exploring every hidden gem and popular spot, my goal was to bring Costa Rica to you through pages that resonate with authenticity and excitement. From uncovering the best surf breaks to sharing a cup of rich, local coffee in quaint mountain towns, I've aimed to offer you not just facts but experiences.

As we wrap up this guide, I hope the adventures and memories you've collected will inspire you to return or explore even further. Remember, every trip you take is a new chapter, and there's always more to discover.

Safe travels and remember, the spirit of Costa Rica will always be with you, encouraging you to explore and enjoy life to the fullest. See you next time!

Made in the USA
Columbia, SC
25 November 2024

47579867R00067